D0729506

The Deficit Problem
in Perspective

The Deficit Problem in Perspective

Richard J. Cebula
Emory University

BOWLING GREEN STATE UNIVERSITY
DISCARDED
LIBRARY

Lexington Books
D.C. Heath and Company/Lexington, Massachusetts/Toronto

JEROME LIBRARY-BOWLING GREEN STATE UNIVERSITY

Library of Congress Cataloging-in-Publication Data

Cebula, Richard J.
    The deficit problem in perspective.

    Includes index.
    1. Budget deficits—United States.   2. Fiscal policy—United States.   3. Budget—Law and
legislation—United States.   I. Title.
HJ2052.C42   1987   339.5'23'0973   86–45792
ISBN 0–669–14303–0 (alk. paper)

Copyright © 1987 by D.C. Heath and Company

All rights reserved. No part of this publication may be reproduced or transmitted in any form
or by any means, electronic or mechanical, including photocopy, recording, or any
information storage or retrieval system, without permission in writing from the publisher.

Published simultaneously in Canada
Printed in the United States of America
International Standard Book Number: 0–669–14303–0
Library of Congress Catalog Card Number: 86–45792

The paper used in this publication meets the minimum requirements of American National
Standard for Information Sciences—Permanence of Paper for Printed Library Materials, ANSI
Z39.48–1984. ∞™

87 88 89 90   8 7 6 5 4 3 2 1

To Christie and David and my Mother and Father, for their love.

Contents

Figures and Tables

Figures

Tables

Preface and Acknowledgments

In recent years the size of the federal budget deficit in the United States has grown rapidly, resulting in a rapidly growing concern for the potentially adverse economic consequences of the federal deficit. Given such a concern, it may be useful to have a basic understanding of deficits, their possible effects, and their cures.

This book is divided into five chapters. Chapter 1 is the introductory chapter, which attempts to define the objective of the book. In chapter 2, the concept of "crowding out" is developed at length. In this chapter, the reader is introduced to basic theories of how deficits may affect the economy. Most of this chapter is entirely accessible to students taking intermediate-level courses. However, one may wish to make the section on "Negative Transactions Crowding Out" optional, as these pages involve calculus and a formal mathematical treatment of macroeconomic stability. In chapter 3, an empirical analysis of the apparent actual effects of deficits upon interest rates in the real world is provided. In chapter 4, the possible usefulness of a balanced-budget amendment to the U.S. Constitution is examined. Various forms of such an amendment are considered, along with drawbacks and limitations of such an amendment. Finally, chapter 5 deals with various other public policies that might be used to control the federal deficit.

This project was undertaken over a period of two years (1985–86). During this period, a number of people have offered useful suggestions. Among these people, I especially wish to thank Dick Muth, Bob Conrad, Mary Beth Walker, and Milton Kafoglis. I am also extremely indebted to Terrell Miller for his extremely capable data assembly and computer assistance. I also wish to thank David Cebula and Christie Cebula for assistance in data assembly. Finally, I wish to acknowledge Mrs. Amy Erbil for her extremely gracious typing efforts.

1
Introduction

I n recent years, concern has grown in the United States over the possible
economic implications of rapidly growing and relatively large (by historical standards, in the United States) federal budget deficits. A federal
budget deficit is simply a situation in which federal government spending is
greater than federal government receipts (principally tax collections). When
the federal government's income falls short of its spending, the U.S. Treasury
must borrow the difference. It is important to stress that the Treasury does
not per se print money to finance a deficit—it merely borrows the money.

The Magnitude of the Deficit

Table 1–1 illustrates the size of the federal government's receipts, outlays,
and budget surpluses or deficits for all fiscal years (FY) since 1939.[1] The
period of seemingly greatest concern commences with, more or less, the
beginning of President Reagan's first term of office. Table 1–1 crudely illustrates what seems to be an enormous surge in the deficit size (when measured in current dollars) beginning in FY 1982.[2]

The degree of concern over the federal deficit is exemplified not only by
daily news stories on the topic (stories that may not only reflect concern
over the deficit, but that may as well contribute to that concern), but also
by various studies which project federal deficits, debt,[3] and interest payments
on the national debt. One of the better known of these studies is the *President's Private Sector Survey on Cost Control* (Grace Commission, 1984).
Table 1–2, which provides actual and projected values for deficits, debt, and
interest payments for the years 1980, 1983, 1985, 1990, 1995, and 2000,
was generated by this 1984 study. As shown, these projections allege that
the deficit in the year 2000 will be thirty-three times the size of the deficit
in 1980; the national debt in the year 2000 will be fourteen times the size
of the national debt in 1980; and total interest payments on the national
debt in the year 2000 will be twenty-nine times the size of those same pay-

Table 1–1
Federal Budget Receipts, Outlays, and Deficits
(in billions of current dollars)

Fiscal Year	Receipts	Outlays	Surplus or Deficit
1940	6.5	9.5	−2.9
1941	8.7	13.7	−4.9
1942	14.6	35.1	−20.5
1943	24.0	78.6	−54.6
1944	43.7	91.3	−47.6
1945	45.2	92.7	−47.6
1946	39.3	55.2	−15.9
1947	38.5	34.5	4.0
1948	41.6	29.8	11.8
1949	39.4	38.8	0.6
1950	39.4	42.6	−3.1
1951	51.6	45.5	6.1
1952	66.2	67.7	−1.5
1953	69.6	76.1	−6.5
1954	69.7	70.9	−1.2
1955	65.5	68.4	−3.0
1956	74.6	70.6	3.9
1957	80.0	76.6	3.4
1958	79.6	82.4	−2.8
1959	79.2	92.1	−12.8
1960	92.5	92.2	0.3
1961	94.4	97.7	−3.3
1962	99.7	106.8	−7.1
1963	106.6	111.3	−4.8
1964	112.6	118.5	−5.9
1965	116.8	118.2	−1.4
1966	130.8	134.5	−3.7
1967	148.8	157.5	−8.6
1968	153.0	178.1	−25.2
1969	186.9	183.6	3.2
1970	192.8	195.6	−2.8
1971	187.1	210.2	−23.0
1972	207.3	230.7	−23.4
1973	230.8	245.6	−14.8
1974	263.2	267.9	−4.7
1975	279.1	324.2	−45.2
1976	298.1	364.5	−66.4
Transition quarter	81.2	94.2	−13.0
1977	355.6	400.5	−44.9
1978	399.7	448.4	−48.6
1979	463.3	491.0	−27.7
1980	517.1	576.7	−59.6
1981	599.3	657.2	−57.9
1982	617.8	728.4	−110.6
1983	600.6	796.0	−195.4
1984	666.5	841.8	−175.4
1985	736.9	944.6	−211.9
1986	793.7	972.2	−178.5

Source: Economic Report of the President, 1986, Table B–73.

Table 1–2
Federal Debt, Deficit, and Interest on Debt
(in billions of current dollars)

Year	Debt	Deficit	Interest on Debt
1980	914.3	59.6	52.5
1983	1,381.9	195.4	87.8
1985	1,823.1	202.8	179.0
1990	3,211.0	386.7	252.3
1995	6,156.7	775.4	540.9
2000	13,020.9	1966.0	1,520.7

Source: The President's Private Sector Survey on Cost Control Washington, D.C.: U.S. Government Printing Office, 1984, pp. 1–2.

ments in 1980. The accuracy of such projections can of course be questioned. However, the fact that such forecasts cause great public concern cannot be.

There are many ways to analyze the magnitudes of the deficit and the national debt. One way is to analyze the deficit and national debt in real terms, that is, analyze these items after adjusting them for inflation. This issue is addressed in chapter 5 of this book. Nonetheless, two brief remarks seem appropriate. First, inflation reduces the value of the national debt and deficits so that the size of the deficit in current dollars per se grossly exaggerates the growth of the real national debt. Second, after adjusting deficits for inflation, they are not all so large as they first appear to be. Nevertheless, the real deficit (in billions of 1982 dollars) has grown measurably since 1980:

1980	−69.55
1981	−117.68
1982	−195.40
1983	−169.09
1984	−196.01
1985	−159.76

An alternative means by which to measure the size of the deficit is to relate it to the level of gross national product (GNP). The GNP level provides an indication of the size of the economy that must finance the deficit. Table 1–3 shows the ratio of the federal budget deficit to the GNP level for the period from 1970 through 1985. Clearly, when measured in this fashion, the federal budget deficit has grown immensely (in relative terms), from an average of 1.818 percent of GNP for the period from 1970 to 1980 to an average of 5.02 percent of GNP for the period from 1981 to 1985. Similar observations can be made with respect to both the national debt and interest payments on the national debt; specifically, the ratio of the national debt to

Table 1–3
The Ratio of the Deficit to GNP
(in percents)

Year	Ratio of Deficit to GNP
1970	0.3
1971	2.1
1972	1.9
1973	1.1
1974	0.3
1975	2.8
1976	3.7
1977	2.3
1978	2.2
1979	1.1
1980	2.2
1981	3.6
1982	6.2
1983	5.2
1984	5.6
1985	4.5

the GNP level and the ratio of interest payments on the national debt to the GNP level are substantially higher during the period from 1981 to 1985 than during the period from 1970 to 1980.

Objective of the Book

The federal deficit, whether measured in current dollars (see table 1–1), in real (constant dollar) terms (see table in preceding section), or relative to the GNP level (see table 1–3), seems to have risen dramatically in recent years. There has indeed been an apparent surge of concern over the possible economic ramifications of the burgeoning federal deficit. Newspaper articles have proclaimed the deficit as the future cause of the death of our republic.[4] Persons such as David Stockman (1986, p. 395) have proclaimed that "the inflation-battered American economy of 1980 was no more sustainable or viable than is the deficit-burdened economy of 1986." Many proclaim the need for passage of a balanced-budget amendment.[5] The Gramm-Rudman-Hollings Act was passed in 1985, allegedly to provide a format for reducing the deficit to zero by 1991.[6] President Reagan has publicly demanded congressional spending cuts and "fiscal responsibility"; indeed, he has publicly chastized Congress for failing to significantly cut domestic spending (see Stockman [1986]).

To many, federal budget deficits are an economic threat. For example, many (but certainly not all) economists argue that when the Treasury borrows to finance a deficit, problems arise. Specifically, when the Treasury borrows, it floods the bond markets with various forms of government bonds. In so doing, the Treasury allegedly pushes market interest rate yields above what they otherwise would be. Given these higher interest rates, many (but not all) economists argue that consumers buy fewer new homes and fewer new automobiles. This means that jobs and income are lost in both the construction and automobile industries. Higher interest rates also discourage firms from investing in new plant and equipment. This means that more jobs and income are lost. In addition, more long-term inflation may result from the reduced rate of capital formation. Furthermore, when interest rates are higher in the United States, the value of the U.S. dollar tends to rise. In turn, this translates into lower exports, higher imports, and higher unemployment in the United States. Some economists and financial analysts argue that additional adverse side effects from deficits are also experienced. To a limited extent, this book (in chapters 3 and 5) will address the validity of these arguments. However, it is important to stress that, while there are many economists who believe in such effects, there are also many who dispute these alleged effects of deficits.

Nevertheless, given these concerns (as well as many other forms of concern) over the possible economic effects of the federal deficit, it may be useful to have a basic understanding of deficits, their possible effects, and their possible cures. Accordingly, the basic purpose of this book is to provide the reader with a rudimentary analysis of: (1) the potential effects of federal budget deficits; (2) the actual apparent effects of federal budget deficits on the U.S. economy; (3) the potential usefulness of a balanced-budget amendment to control the deficit; and (4) the potential usefulness of the Gramm-Rudman-Hollings Act and various other public economic policies to control the deficit.

This book is broken into five chapters. Chapter 1 is the introduction, which defines the objective and scope of this book. In chapter 2, the concept of crowding out is developed. In this chapter, the reader is introduced to most of the basic theories of how deficits may affect the economy. Most of this chapter is entirely accessible to students taking intermediate-level courses. However, one may wish to make the section on "negative transactions crowding out" optional, as this section involves calculus and a formal mathematical treatment of macroeconomic stability. In chapter 3, an empirical analysis of the apparent actual effects of federal deficits upon interest rates in the real world is provided. For this chapter, a basic knowledge of regression techniques would be helpful, although not absolutely essential. In chapter 4, the possible usefulness of a balanced-budget amendment to the U.S. Constitution is examined. Various forms of such an amendment are considered, along with possible drawbacks and limitations. Finally, chapter 5 deals with various other public policies that might be used to control the federal deficit. These policies include tax policies, spending policies, monetary policies, and legislation (such as the Gramm-Rudman-Hollings Act). The contents of chapters 4 and 5 should be easily accessible to a wide variety of readers and especially appealing to students of economics and political science.

Notes

1. A federal budget surplus is a situation in which federal government receipts exceed federal government outlays.

2. It is interesting to note the finding by Waud (1985, p. 516) that "the existence of a lagged private sector response to tax rate change that exceeds the relevant time horizon for political decision makers is conducive to the existence of a budget deficit bias."

3. Stated simply, the national debt represents the outstanding borrowings of the federal government.

4. See, for example, the article by Figgie International entitled "Of Debt, Deficits, and the Death of a Republic," *The New York Times,* April 20, 1986, F-9.

5. This topic will be addressed in chapter 4.

6. This topic will be addressed in chapter 5.

References

Council of Economic Advisors. 1986. *Economic Report of the President, 1986.* Washington, D.C.: U.S. Government Printing Office.

Figgie International. 1986. "Of Debt, Deficits, and the Death of a Republic." *The New York Times,* April 20, F-9.

Grace Commission. 1984. *The President's Private Sector Survey on Cost Control.* Washington, D.C.: U.S. Government Printing Office.

Stockman, D. 1986. *The Triumph of Politics.* New York: Harper and Row.

Waud, R.N. 1985. "Politics, Deficits, and the Laffer Curve." *Public Choice* 47:509–17.

2
Crowding Out and Fiscal Policy Effectiveness

M uch of the current debate in the United States about the effects of our extraordinarily large federal budget deficits (past, present, and projected) centers around the allegedly adverse economic impact of such deficits. In turn, the adverse economic impact of budget deficits is probably most frequently associated with the phenomenon known as *crowding out,* although the alleged inflationary impact of deficits has received considerable attention in recent years (see, for example, Dwyer [1982]).

Crowding out, in general, refers to the effects of expansionary fiscal actions on private sector spending (principally, private investment and consumption outlays). As Carlson and Spencer (1975, p. 3) have observed:

> if an increase in government demand ($\Delta G > 0$), financed by either taxes or debt issuance to the public, fails to stimulate total economic activity, the private sector is . . . "crowded out" by the government action.

In perhaps its simplest form, crowding out refers to the offsetting changes in private investment and consumption outlays resulting when an expansionary fiscal action acts to raise the interest rate. As will be demonstrated in the following section, however, the means by which private investment and/or consumption may be crowded out by the expansionary fiscal policy can be rather complex.

This chapter summarizes and analyzes the topic of crowding out at the analytical level. It begins with a brief description of crowding out. Next, various theories or interpretations of crowding out are examined. This material will serve as a useful backdrop for the empirical analyses provided in chapters three through five.

Crowding Out: General Observations

As already noted, crowding out implies that increased government spending displaces private sector spending. Let ΔG represent increased government spending and ΔZ represent decreased private sector spending. Utilizing this notation, crowding out may be classified in three different ways. To begin with, if

$$|\Delta G| = |\Delta Z|, \tag{2.1}$$

then the degree of crowding out is said to be *complete*. On the other hand, if

$$|\Delta G| > |\Delta Z|, \tag{2.2}$$

then *partial* crowding out is said to occur. Finally, if

$$|\Delta G| > |\Delta Z| = 0, \tag{2.3}$$

then *zero* crowding out is said to exist.

At the empirical level, the possibility that crowding out may be complete can be traced to the studies by Anderson and Jordan (1968) and Keran (1969 and 1970), although the recent study by Batten and Thornton (1985) deserves attention as well. Other empirical studies, such as studies by Abrams and Schmitz (1978), Arestis (1979), Zahn (1978), and Cebula, Carlos, and Koch (1981), have found evidence of only partial crowding out. Still other studies, such as Hoelscher (1983) and Evans (1985), suggest that crowding out may be statistically unimportant. These empirical studies use different techniques, examine different variables, and consider different time periods. Thus, the fact that they generate varying results should come as no surprise. In part, the fact that these results differ so much is traceable to the fact that some empirical (as well as some theoretical) analyses examine the crowding out impact of government spending, whereas other studies examine the crowding out impact of government budget deficits. Although these two phenomena (that is, government expenditures and government budget deficits) are obviously closely related, they clearly are not synonomous. Accordingly, in the analysis that follows, as well as in chapter three, we shall endeavor to distinguish between (1) the crowding out effect of government spending increases per se and (2) the crowding out effect of government budget deficits or borrowing per se.

Crowding Out in the Crude Classical System

The basic elements of the crude Classical system are lucidly developed in Patinkin (1948 and 1965). To demonstrate the crowding out phenomenon in the crude Classical system, the following system of equations should be considered:

$$Y = C + I + G \tag{2.4}$$

$$C = C(Yd, i), \; 1 > \partial C/\partial Yd > 0, \; \partial C/\partial i < 0 \tag{2.5}$$

$$I = I(Y, i), \; 1 > \partial I/\partial Y > 0, \; \partial I/\partial i < 0 \tag{2.6}$$

$$G = \overline{G} \tag{2.7}$$

$$T = \overline{T} \tag{2.8}$$

$$Ms/P = Md \tag{2.9}$$

$$Md = Md(Y), \; Md'\,(Y) > 0 \tag{2.10}$$

$$Ms = \overline{M} \tag{2.11}$$

$$Y = Y(N, \overline{K}), \; Y'(N,\overline{K}) > 0, \; Y''(N,\overline{K}) < 0 \tag{2.12}$$

$$ND = ND(W/P), \; ND'(W/P) < 0 \tag{2.13}$$

$$NS = NS(W/P), \; NS'(W/P) > 0 \tag{2.14}$$

$$W, P = \text{perfectly flexible} \tag{2.15}$$

$$NS = ND = N, \tag{2.16}$$

where it is also assumed that

$$\partial S/\partial Yd > \partial I/\partial Y, \tag{2.17}$$

and where Y is real GNP; C is aggregate real consumption; I is aggregate real investment; G is aggregate real government spending; Yd is aggregate real disposable income; i is interest rate; $\overline{G}$ is exogenous real government spending; T is aggregate real tax collections; $\overline{T}$ is exogenous real tax level;

Ms is nominal money stock; *P* is aggregate price level; *Md* is aggregate real money demand; $\overline{M}$ is exogenous nominal money stock; *N* is employment of labor (units of labor employed); $\overline{K}$ is fixed capital stock; *ND* is aggregate labor demand; *W* is nominal wage rate; *NS* is aggregate labor supply; and *S* is aggregate saving.

The system shown in equations 2.4 through 2.17 is but one possible interpretation of the crude Classical system. For example, it is not uncommon for the interest rate to be omitted from the consumption function or for the GNP level to be omitted from the investment function in the crude Classical system. Nevertheless, the outcomes and critical traits of the system conform to the norm (see, for example, Patinkin [1948 and 1965]). Next, we observe that the condition shown in equation 2.17 is sufficient, in this system, to generate a negatively sloped *IS* curve. Moreover, the fact that money demand does not depend upon the interest rate implies a vertical *LM* curve. Finally, the labor market in this system, since it is characterized by perfect flexibility of both money wages (*W*) and prices (*P*), generates a perfectly vertical aggregate supply curve.

Figure 2–1 shows the economy to be initially in equilibrium at interest rate *i'* and real GNP level *YF*, given $G = \overline{G}$ and $T = \overline{T}$, and hence *IS* curve *IS'*. If the level of government spending is to be increased, we must somehow finance the spending increase. This notion may be easily described with the use of a *government budget constraint*. Essentially, in its simplest form, a government budget constraint describes the relationship between the level of government spending and the sources of funds required to finance that spending. One possible form of a government budget constraint is shown by

$$G - T = \Delta Ms + \Delta B, \tag{2.18}$$

where ΔB represents bond sales by the Treasury to the public to help finance $(G - T)$. In order to describe the crowding out effect of fiscal policy per se, it is appropriate here to hold

$$\Delta Ms = 0 \tag{2.19}$$

Hence, equation 2.18 becomes

$$G - T = \Delta B \tag{2.20}$$

To simplify matters further, we demonstrate crowding out in the crude Classical system by holding

$$\Delta T = 0 \tag{2.21}$$

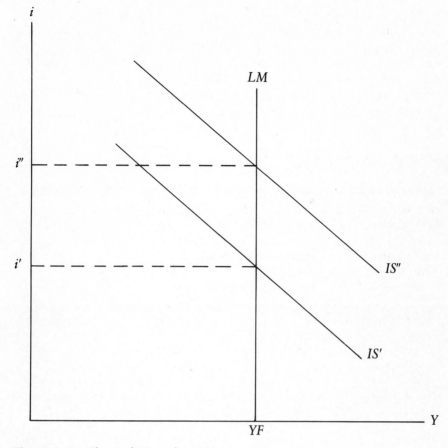

Figure 2–1. Classical Crowding Out

Accordingly, if we increase government spending by ΔG, then

$$\Delta G = \Delta B \qquad (2.22)$$

In terms of figure 2–1, this bond-financed fiscal policy has the effect of shifting the *IS* curve from *IS'* to *IS"*. Clearly, the new *IS-LM* equilibrium corresponds to the higher interest rate *i"* and the unchanged real GNP level *YF*. Hence, in this crude Classical system, crowding out is said to be complete. That is, it follows that

$$|\Delta G| = |\Delta C| + |\Delta I| \qquad (2.23)$$

As the Treasury sold new bonds to finance ΔG, the interest rate in the economy was pushed upwards. In turn, the levels of C and I were both reduced. Since the equilibrium real GNP level was left unchanged, government spending crowded out private sector spending dollar for dollar. Moreover, the fiscal policy action simply redistributed GNP from the private sector of the economy to the public sector of the economy.

Crowding Out in the Crude Keynesian Model

The so-called crude Keynesian system may be described by the following:

$$Y = C + I + G \tag{2.24}$$

$$C = C(Yd), 1 > C'\,(Yd) > 0 \tag{2.25}$$

$$I = \bar{I} \tag{2.26}$$

$$G = \bar{G} \tag{2.27}$$

$$T = \bar{T} \tag{2.28}$$

$$Ms/P = Md \tag{2.29}$$

$$Md = Md(Y, i), \partial Md/\partial Y > 0, \partial MD/\partial i < 0 \tag{2.30}$$

$$Ms = \bar{M} \tag{2.31}$$

$$Y = Y(N, \bar{K}), Y'(N,\bar{K}) > 0, Y''(N,\bar{K}) < 0 \tag{2.32}$$

$$ND = ND(W/P), ND'(W/P) < 0 \tag{2.33}$$

$$NS = NS(W/P), NS'(W/P) > 0 \tag{2.34}$$

$$W = \text{rigid downwards} \tag{2.35}$$

$$W = \text{flexible upwards at full employment} \tag{2.36}$$

$$P = \text{flexible upwards and downwards} \tag{2.37}$$

$$N = ND'(W/P) \tag{2.38}$$

The system summarized in equations 2.24 through 2.38 represents an extreme interpretation of the macro-model in *The General Theory of Employment, Interest, and Money* by John M. Keynes (1936).

In the system shown in figure 2–1, the *IS* curve is perfectly vertical, due to the absence of an interest rate effect in the commodity market. The *LM* curve, however, unlike that in the crude Classical system, is positively sloped. Moreover, the aggregate supply schedule is upward sloping to the point of full employment (*YF*) (and then perfectly vertical above that point).

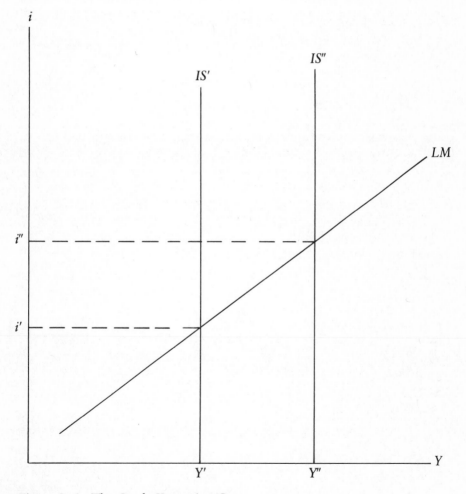

Figure 2–2. The Crude Keynesian Case

Figure 2–2 illustrates the economy at an initial *IS-LM* equilibrium at interest rate i' and real GNP level Y', given $G = \overline{G}$, $T = \overline{T}$, and hence *IS* curve *IS'*. If the government spending level is increased and solely financed by Treasury bond sales to the public, then the *IS* curve shifts rightwards to *IS''*. The economy then moves to real GNP level Y'' and interest rate i''. Notice that, given the interest insensitivity of commodity market demand, the higher interest rate resulting from the policy cannot affect (that is, reduce) private sector spending. In this system, private sector spending is simply not crowded out at all by the expansionary fiscal policy. The reader can readily demonstrate that, even allowing for the effects of a rising aggregate price level on the *LM* curve, the crude Keynesian case is associated with *zero* crowding out. This is because, in this crude Keynesian case, as the price level increases and the *LM* curve then shifts upwards, the *IS-LM* equilibrium still corresponds to the same, new real GNP level, namely, real GNP Y''.

Keynes, Expectations, and Confidence

The previous section of this chapter sketches out a scenario wherein the crude Keynesian system generates zero crowding out. In this section, a more moderate version of Keynesian system is considered, one which allows for a marginal efficiency of capital and the issues of public confidence and expectations.

Keynes (1936, p. 120) seemed somewhat concerned that government spending could adversely affect public confidence. In turn, he saw the effect of the government spending program as potentially increasing liquidity preference (Md) and decreasing the marginal efficiency of capital. These possible impacts from a government spending program are focused upon in figure 2–3, where the *IS* curve is negatively sloped and where the *LM* curve is positively sloped.[1]

The economy is shown initially in figure 2–3 to be in equilibrium at the intersection of curves *LM* and *IS'*, where, given $G = \overline{G}$, the interest rate is i', and the real GNP level is Y'. Now let G rise by ΔG to the level $\overline{G} + \Delta G$. This shifts the *IS* curve from *IS'* to *IS''* and generates a new *IS-LM* equilibrium at $Y = Y''$ and $i = i''$. However, as a result of the rising government spending level, liquidity preference is increased, which shifts the *LM* curve leftwards, and the marginal efficiency of capital is decreased, which then shifts the *IS* curve leftwards as well.

Clearly, as the *LM* and *IS* curves both shift leftwards, the real GNP level is being reduced below Y''. Depending upon the relative shifts of the *LM* and *IS* curve, the degree of crowding out could theoretically be either partial or complete.[2] Clearly, the results shown in figure 2–3 differ sharply from those in figure 2–2.

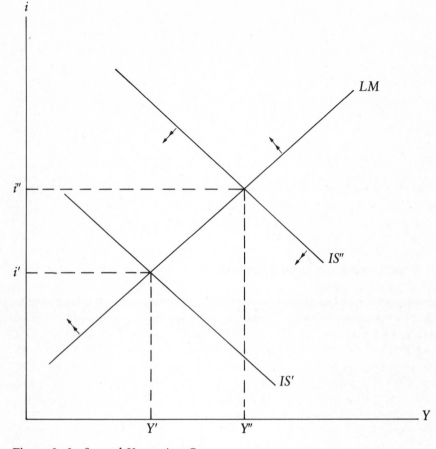

Figure 2–3. Second Keynesian Case

Transactions Crowding Out

Perhaps the simplest and best known form of crowding out is that known as *transactions crowding out*. For simplicity, this concept may be examined with the use of the following commodity market:

$$Y = C + I + G \tag{2.39}$$

$$C = C(Yd, i) = a + bYd - ei \tag{2.40}$$

$$I = I(Y, i) = \bar{I} + fY - hi \tag{2.41}$$

$$G = \overline{G} \tag{2.42}$$

$$T = \overline{T} \tag{2.43}$$

The equilibrium GNP in this market is given by

$$Y = \frac{a - b\overline{T} - ei + \overline{I} - hi + \overline{G}}{1 - b - f} \tag{2.44}$$

The simple government spending multiplier corresponding to system (2.39) − (2.43), $\Delta Y/\Delta G$, is given by

$$\frac{\Delta Y}{\Delta G} = \frac{1}{1 - b - f} \tag{2.45}$$

The money market is given by equations 2.29 through 2.31, whereas the labor market is given by equations 2.32 through 2.38.

Refer now to figure 2–4, where the economy is shown to be initially in equilibrium at interest rate i^* and real GNP level Y^*; that is, at the intersection of curves IS^* and LM^*. The level of government spending along IS^* is given by $\overline{G}$. Now let the government spending level rise by the amount ΔG. Assume that this increased government spending is financed solely by treasury bond sales to the public:

$$\Delta G = \Delta B \tag{2.46}$$

The rise in government spending shifts the IS curve rightwards to IS^{**}; specifically, the IS curve is shifted rightwards by the amount

$$\Delta G\left(\frac{1}{1 - b - f}\right) \tag{2.47}$$

However, whereas the IS curve shifts rightwards by this amount, the level of GNP cannot rise by as much as this amount. This is because as the level of GNP begins to increase, the aggregate demand for money also increases. In turn, a rising aggregate demand for money elevates the interest rate and, in so doing, reduces both investment and consumption. Thus, due to the expansion brought on by $\Delta G (\Delta G > 0)$, the transactions demand for money is increased, which in turn raises interest rates and thereby discourages investment and consumption as the economy moves along curve LM^* from coordinates (Y^*, i^*) to coordinates (Y^{**}, i^{**}).[3]

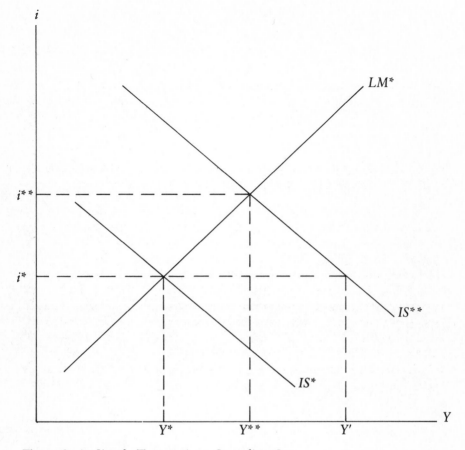

Figure 2–4. Simple Transactions Crowding Out

The change in GNP that would have occurred as a result of ΔG, in the absence of transactions crowding out, is given by

$$Y' - Y^* \qquad (2.48)$$

The actual change in GNP that occurs is given by

$$Y^{**} - Y^* \qquad (2.49)$$

Hence, transactions crowding out results in partial crowding out in the amount of

$$Y' - Y^{**} = (Y' - Y^*) - (Y^{**} - Y^*) \qquad (2.50)$$

In closing this section, it is clear that the extent of the partial crowding out resulting from transactions crowding out depends significantly upon the relative slopes of the *IS* and *LM* curves. The interested reader is referred to the theoretical paper by Meyer (1983) and to the empirical study by Sullivan (1976). The latter actually provides an empirical estimate of the slopes of these two curves.

The Case of Ultrarationality

Yet another theory (explanation) of crowding out has been formulated by David and Scadding (1974). David and Scadding assume *ultrarationality* on the part of households. Households are portrayed as viewing the government sector and the corporate sector of the economy as, in effect, extensions of themselves; that is, as vehicles for the pursuit of their private interests. Accordingly, a government budget deficit presumably displaces an equal amount of private investment because deficit financing is interpreted as public investment and therefore as a substitute for private investment since households regard private investment and public investment as merely alternative means of achieving an increased flow of future consumption benefits.

Ultrarationality may be illustrated in part with the use of figure 2–5. The economy is shown initially to be in equilibrium at the intersection of curves *IS'* and *LM*, corresponding to real GNP level *Y'* and interest rate *i'*. Let government spending rise by ΔG, which amount is financed by borrowing from the public:

$$\Delta G = \Delta B \tag{2.51}$$

This policy initially shifts the *IS* curve rightwards from *IS'* to *IS''*. However, the equal decline in private investment shifts the *IS* curve leftwards from *IS''* back to *IS'*. Thus, as we have seen elsewhere, the implication is complete crowding out.

It should be noted that this same final conclusion, namely, that of complete crowding out due to ultrarationality, is obtained if the increased government spending is financed through taxes on households. In such a case, the tax-financed expenditure increase presumably displaces private consumption outlays because the expenditure increase is evaluated in terms of its current consumption benefits and will be simply substituted by households for private consumer outlays.

Whether the increased government expenditure is financed through bond sales to the public or through increased taxes on households, the outcome is the same: complete crowding out. The ultimate impact of the policy will be to merely redistribute the economy's output from the private sector (cor-

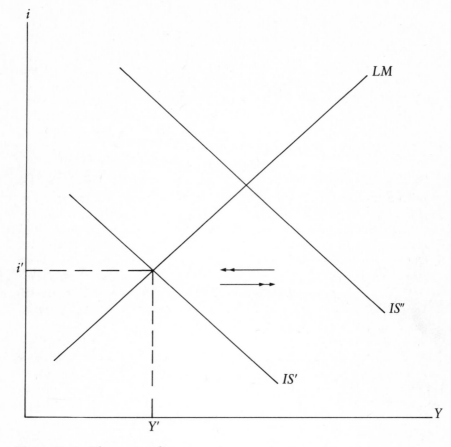

Figure 2–5. Ultrarationality

porate and/or household) of the economy to the government sector of the economy. Actually, as shown in figure 2–5 this final outcome is somewhat similar to that obtained in the crude Classical system, except that the mechanism in the present case is ultrarationality, whereas the mechanism is the interest rate (at full employment) in the crude Classical case.[4]

Two brief comments may now be in order. First, one might wish to question the underlying tenet of ultrarationality; that is, the perfect substitutability in the eyes of the household sector of, say, public investment for private investment. Second, if there were, for example, only a limited degree of substitutability of public investment for private investment, then a so-modified form of ultrarationality might conceivably be inferred as leading to only partial crowding out.

Financial Crowding Out

Financial crowding out is sometimes confused with transactions crowding out.[5] This confusion may stem from the role that the interest rate, an obvious category of financial variable, plays in transactions crowding out. As the following illustrates, however, financial crowding out deals with a quite different set of phenomena from transactions crowding out.

In order to illustrate financial crowding out, refer to figure 2–6, where the economy is shown to be initially in equilibrium at the intersection of curves *IS** and *LM*, where the interest rate is *i** and the real GNP level is *Y**. Let the level of government spending rise by Δ*G*; furthermore, let Δ*G* be financed by treasury bond sales to the public. The increased government

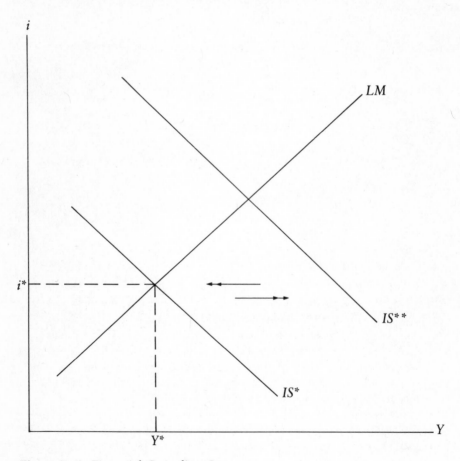

Figure 2–6. Financial Crowding Out

spending level shifts the *IS* curve from *IS** to *IS***. Nobel laureate Milton Friedman (1970 and 1971), and other economists as well, has argued that this shift in the *IS* curve is only temporary, however.

More specifically, according to the financial crowding out hypothesis, investment presumably depends not only upon the interest rate, but also upon the supply of savings available for firms to borrow for investment purposes, *F*. Thus

$$I = I(i, F), \tag{2.52}$$

where

$$\frac{\partial I}{\partial i} < 0, \frac{\partial I}{\partial F} > 0 \tag{2.53}$$

If government spending rises by ΔG and if the increased spending is solely financed by bond sales to the public so that[6]

$$\Delta G = \Delta B, \tag{2.54}$$

then it may be argued that the deficit (ΔB) absorbs ΔG worth of savings (*F*) that would have otherwise presumably been funneled to firms for private investment. Accordingly, it is argued that private investment spending declines by an amount equal in absolute value to $\Delta G = \Delta B$:

$$|\Delta I| = |\Delta G| = |\Delta B| \tag{2.55}$$

This sequence of events in turn allegedly implies that the *IS* curve will then shift leftwards from *IS*** back to *IS**. Consequently, the degree of the crowding out is complete, and the value of the government spending multiplier (dY/dG) is zero. As seen previously in this chapter,[7] the net final impact of the fiscal action is not to alter the final real GNP level, but rather to merely alter the composition of real GNP, with investment in this case simply being replaced, dollar-for-dollar, by government spending.

Portfolio Crowding Out and the Wealth Effect

Yet another theory of crowding out involves *portfolio crowding out and real net wealth effects*. Many economists, including Patinkin (1965), argue that the private sector demand for both commodities and money is influenced, in part, by household real net wealth. Consider, for example, the following two simple relationships:

$$C = C(Yd, i, W^H) \tag{2.56}$$

$$Md = Md(Y, i, W^H), \tag{2.57}$$

where W^H = household real net wealth, and where

$$1 > \frac{\partial C}{\partial Yd} > 0, \frac{\partial C}{\partial i} < 0, \frac{\partial C}{\partial W^H} > 0 \tag{2.58}$$

$$\frac{\partial Md}{\partial Y} > 0, \frac{\partial Md}{\partial i} < 0, \frac{\partial Md}{\partial W^H} > 0 \tag{2.59}$$

Given the behavior described in equations 2.56 through 2.59, let us proceed to examine a simple form of portfolio crowding out.

Refer now to figure 2–7, where the economy is initially shown to be in equilibrium at the intersection of curves IS' and LM', corresponding to real GNP level Y' and interest rate i'. The curve IS' is predicated upon the government spending level $\overline{G}$. Now let government spending rise by ΔG, and let ΔG be financed solely by sales of bonds to the public. The initial impact of this fiscal policy action of course is to shift the IS curve to the right, say, to IS''. This outcome gives the initial impression of a rise in the interest rate (to i'') and a rise in the real GNP level (to Y'') as well. Thus, at the end of the first time period, "period 1," it seems that $\Delta i > 0$ and $\Delta Y > 0$, as a result of the fiscal action. Of course, the effects of the fiscal action in question at this point reflect a partial transactions crowding out to the extent of $Y^* - Y''$ in figure 2–7.

Whatever bonds the government sells in order to finance its first (initial)-period deficit have no impact on C or Md until the next time period (or "period 2"). In other words, if the government sells bonds to the public in order to finance a first-period deficit (ΔG), these same bonds will become a part of households' real net wealth at the beginning of the next (second) time period.

In any event, it is apparent that, at some point, the household sector's real net wealth rises due to the increase in the household sector's holdings of government bonds. This in turn has two sets of effects upon the economy: (1) It raises consumption spending and thereby shifts the IS curve to the right (upwards), and (2) it raises money demand (real) and thereby shifts the LM curve to the left (upwards). On the one hand, the impact of the IS curve shift is to raise the GNP level (and interest rates as well, of course).

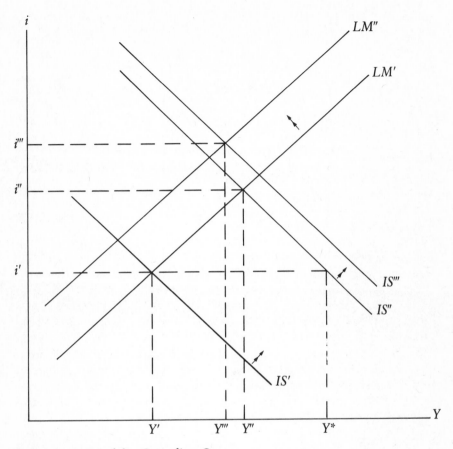

Figure 2–7. Portfolio Crowding Out

On the other hand, the impact of the *LM* curve shift is to lower the GNP level (while pushing interest rates upwards).

Whether the *LM* curve will shift to the left more than the *IS* curve will shift to the right is not known on a priori grounds. One theoretically possible outcome from the described shifting of these two curves is illustrated in figure 2–7, where the *IS* curve is shown to have shifted from *IS"* to *IS'''*, and where the *LM* curve is shown to have shifted from *LM'* to *LM"*. Given curves *IS'''* and *LM"*, the economy is shown to be in equilibrium at real GNP level *Y'''* and interest rate *i'''*.

Thus, as shown in figure 2–7, it appears that wealth effects such as those shown in equations 2.56 through 2.59 might potentially lead to partial portfolio crowding out. Nevertheless, the net effect of the fiscal action in question (where $\Delta G = \Delta B$), in the context of the wealth effect, is still ambiguous.[8]

Portfolio Substitution Crowding Out

Klein (1972) has provided another possible source (form) of crowding out. It is referred to as *portfolio substitution crowding out*. This hypothesis essentially argues that new government bond issues, because of their substitutability for commodities and money, affect the locations of both *IS* and *LM* curves and hence may significantly alter the effectiveness of fiscal policy actions upon the economy.

Refer to figure 2–8, where the economy is initially in equilibrium at the

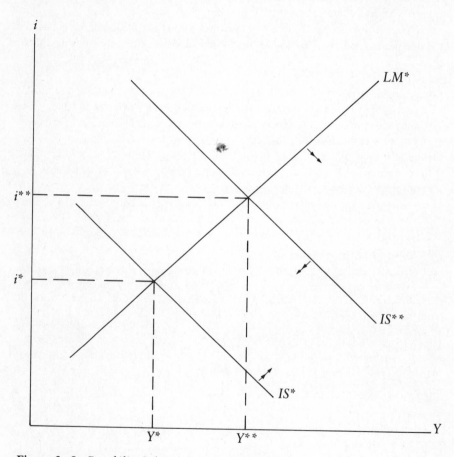

Figure 2–8. Portfolio Substitution Crowding Out

intersection of curves *IS** and *LM**, corresponding to real GNP *Y** and interest rate *i**. We begin by increasing the government spending level by ΔG and by financing the spending increase by a sale of new government bonds to, say, the nonbank public. This has the initial impact of shifting the *IS* curve rightwards from *IS** to *IS***. In turn, the economy appears to move from real GNP level *Y** to real GNP level *Y*** and from interest rate *i** to interest rate *i***. Hence, the initial impacts of the policy appear to be

$$\Delta Y > 0, \Delta i > 0 \qquad (2.60)$$

Naturally, in moving from coordinates (Y^*, i^*) to coordinates (Y^{**}, i^{**}), the economy experiences partial transactions crowding out (see figure 2–4).

Now consider the alleged effects of ΔB according to Klein. Klein argues that the nonbank public, after the government has borrowed the funds required to finance the deficit and after the government has spent those funds, has as much money as before. However, it also has additional (and new) government bonds. As these new bonds were being issued to the nonbank public, they were competing with commodities and money for a place in the portfolios of the nonbank public. The successful sale of the newly issued government bonds implies a substitution of these new bonds for commodities and money. Hence, the demand for commodities presumably must decline, as must the demand for money. In turn, this fact implies a leftward shifting of the *IS* curve and a rightward shifting of the *LM* curve. Klein argues that if the new *IS-LM* equilibrium lies to the left of real GNP level *Y*** in figure 2–8 (and it may or may not), then partial crowding out (of the portfolio substitution variety) occurs. This is, of course, in addition to the obvious transactions crowding out (partial) that also occurs.

Klein also examines wealth effects in his analysis. When he integrates wealth effects with his substitution crowding out hypothesis, he derives nine different possible combinations of net shifts in the *IS* and *LM* curves being generated by an expansionary, bond-financed fiscal action. He does not evaluate the relative likelihoods of these nine possible outcomes; that is, he does not indicate which outcomes are less likely to occur or which are more likely to occur. Nor does he examine the stability implications of these various possible alternatives. However, several of the outcome possibilities are shown to be compatible with a partial crowding out effect.

Negative Transactions Crowding Out

It is commonplace in conventional macroeconomic models to assume that consumption and/or investment is inversely related to the interest rate. However, a number of recent empirical studies, for example, studies by Weber

(1970 and 1975), Yarrow (1975), and Izenson (1983), have cast at least some doubt upon the validity of these two very familiar assumptions. Moreover, without accepting or rejecting the validity of these empirical findings (especially those by Weber and Yarrow), Cebula (1976) has examined some of the potential implications of the findings for public policy effectiveness. The findings in Cebula (1976) have been extended somewhat in Wang (1980), Cebula (1980), and Hwang and Yu (1984). Nevertheless, no one has as yet expressly addressed the implications of the various empirical findings in Weber (1970 and 1975), Yarrow (1975), and Izenson (1983) for the issue of crowding out per se. Such an analysis follows, however.

Weber has empirically examined the responsiveness of consumption expenditures to changes in the interest rate. His empirical results imply that consumption expenditures are (on balance) *directly* a function of the interest rate. As Weber (1970, p. 600) observes:

> When the rate of interest increases, consumers have the opportunity to maintain the same level of consumption in the future with less saving today. Consequently, they increase current consumption in response to the interest rate increase.

Moreover, the second study by Weber (1975) generates the same essential conclusion; in particular, Weber (1975, p. 857) has found that

> an increase in the weighted average of current and past nominal interest rates would increase consumer expenditures on both nondurables and durables. This finding is in accord with . . . my earlier study of consumption.

In an altogether separate vein, Yarrow (1975, p. 582) has argued that

> the growth rate of the firm, and hence its level of investment, may be an *increasing* function of the rate of interest. . . . Such behavior is said to be a characteristic of the growth-maximizing firm (as opposed to the profit-maximizing firm).

Yarrow's (1975) analysis is both theoretical and empirical in nature.

Moreover, the study by Izenson (1983) offers empirical support for the notion that investment is an increasing function of the interest rate. Izenson examines three different regressions. In all three cases, Izenson (1983, p. 137) finds that

> The coefficient on the interest rate variable (*INR*) is positive and significant far beyond the 0.01 level; this strongly confirms Yarrow's suspicions that the rate of investment might be positively linked with the rate of interest, for the growth maximizing firm.

Without per se rejecting or accepting the findings of Weber (1970 and 1975), Yarrow (1975), and Izenson (1983) as either valid or invalid, this section of the chapter examines the theoretical implications of these findings for the crowding out issue. The analysis that follows generates what is to be referred to here as *negative transactions crowding out.*

The basic model is given by:

$$Y = C + I + G \tag{2.61}$$

$$C = C(Yd, i) \tag{2.62}$$

$$I = I(Y, i) \tag{2.63}$$

$$G = \overline{G} \tag{2.64}$$

$$T = \overline{T} \tag{2.65}$$

$$Ms/P = Md \tag{2.66}$$

$$Ms = \overline{M} \tag{2.67}$$

$$Md = Md(Y, i) \tag{2.68}$$

As has generally been done, for simplicity, variations in the aggregate price level are ignored. While the economy summarized in equations 2.61 through 2.68 is a closed system, the analysis can be easily applied to the case of an open system as well. Indeed, this shall briefly be done later on in this section of the chapter.

In accord with Weber (1970 and 1975), it is assumed here that

$$\frac{\partial C}{\partial i} > 0 \tag{2.69}$$

In accord with the aforementioned studies by Yarrow (1975) and Izenson (1983), it is also assumed here that

$$\frac{\partial I}{\partial i} > 0 \tag{2.70}$$

The remaining restrictions on the partial derivatives in the system are as follows:

$$1 > \frac{\partial C}{\partial Yd} > 0 \tag{2.71}$$

$$1 > \frac{\partial I}{\partial Y} > 0 \qquad (2.72)$$

$$\partial Md/\partial Y > 0, \; \partial Md/\partial i < 0 \qquad (2.73)$$

Hereafter, subscripted terms will denote partial differentiation. Accordingly, the slope of the *IS* curve is then given by

$$\frac{(1 - C_Y - I_Y)}{(C_i + I_i)} \qquad (2.74)$$

In addition, the slope of the *LM* curve, given $dP = 0$, is then given by

$$-\frac{Md_Y}{Md_i} > 0 \qquad (2.75)$$

At this juncture, it is appropriate to briefly examine the notion of "economic stability." In his classic article entitled "Liquidity Preference and the Theory of Interest and Money," Professor Franco Modigliani analyzes the *IS-LM* framework in great detail. Among other things, Modigliani (1944, p. 63) observes that, if an economic system is stable, then

each variable approaches some definite value which it will maintain in time until there occurs some change in the form of [a] functional relationship or in some parameter.

Working within the context of a simple two-market (commodity and money markets) economy, where the markets are characterized by conventional forms of economic behavior, Modigliani (1944, p. 64) demonstrates that stability of an economic system requires that the slope of the *IS* curve be algebraically smaller than the slope of the *LM* curve. This *IS-LM* stability condition has come to be accepted as valid for *most* macroeconomic systems. However, this standard *IS-LM* stability condition does not apply to the system in this section of chapter 2. To demonstrate this fact, follow the analysis in Cebula (1976) and begin by taking the total differentials of the following two summary equations:

$$Y = C(Yd, i) + I(Y, i) + \overline{G} \qquad (2.76)$$

$$\overline{M}/P = Md(Y, i), \qquad (2.77)$$

where, by definition,

$$Yd = Y - \overline{T} \tag{2.78}$$

and where

$$dP = 0 \tag{2.79}$$

by assumption (merely to simplify the analysis).

The total differentials of equations 2.76 and 2.77 are given, respectively, by equations 2.80 and 2.81:

$$dY = C_Y dY + C_i di + I_Y dY + I_i di + d\overline{G} \tag{2.80}$$

$$d\overline{M} = Md_Y dY + Md_i di \tag{2.81}$$

Rearranging the terms in equations 2.80 and 2.81 yields, respectively, equations 2.82 and 2.83:

$$-d\overline{G} = (C_Y + I_Y - 1)dY + (C_i + I_i)di \tag{2.82}$$

$$d\overline{M} = Md_Y dY + Md_i di \tag{2.83}$$

The Routh-Hurwitz stability condition requires that

$$\begin{vmatrix} (C_Y + I_Y - 1) & (C_i + I_i) \\ Md_Y & Md_i \end{vmatrix} > 0 \tag{2.84}$$

The expanded determinant is given by

$$(C_Y + I_Y - 1)(Md_i) - (C_i + I_i)(Md_Y) > 0 \tag{2.85}$$

Multiplying through by (-1) yields

$$(1 - C_Y - I_Y)(Md_i) + (C_i + I_i)(Md_Y) < 0 \tag{2.86}$$

Given $(C_i + I_i) > 0$, equation 2.86 may be rearranged to generate

$$\frac{(1 - C_Y - I_Y)}{(C_i + I_i)} > -\frac{Md_Y}{Md_i} > 0 \tag{2.87}$$

That is, in this economic system, the condition for *IS-LM* stability is that the slope of the *IS* curve must exceed that of the *LM* curve:

$$\text{slope } IS > \text{slope } LM > 0 \tag{2.88}$$

Clearly, this stability condition differs from the stability condition derived by Modigliani (1944). Obviously, this change in the stability condition is exclusively the result of the new behavioral condition that $(C_i + I_i) > 0$.

Thus, the assumptions that $C_i > 0$ and $I_i > 0$ imply that, in order to generate *IS-LM* stability, the *IS* curve is positively sloped and steeper than the *LM* curve. A stable *IS-LM* equilibrium corresponding to condition (2.87) is shown in figure 2–9, at the intersection of curves *IS'* and *LM*.

Now briefly consider an open economy such as

$$Y = C + I + G + X - R \tag{2.89}$$

The additions to the aforementioned closed system are described by

$$X = \overline{X} \tag{2.90}$$

$$R = R(Y) \tag{2.91}$$

where X is real exports, R is real imports, X-R is the balance of trade (in real terms), and where

$$1 > R'(Y) > 0 \tag{2.92}$$

In this system, *IS-LM* stability requires that

$$\frac{1 - C_Y - I_Y + R_Y}{C_i + I_i} > -\frac{Md_Y}{Md_i} > 0 \tag{2.93}$$

Thus, as in the closed system, *IS-LM* stability requires that the slope of the *IS* curve be positive and greater than that of the *LM* curve. To confirm condition (2.93), the reader should follow the procedure illustrated above in equations 2.80 through 2.87.

Returning to the closed economy, refer once again to figure 2–9, where curves *IS'* and *LM* intersect at real GNP level Y' and interest rate i'. Let government spending rise by ΔG, with the increase being financed by bond sales to the public. Thus, we once again have

$$\Delta G = \Delta B \tag{2.94}$$

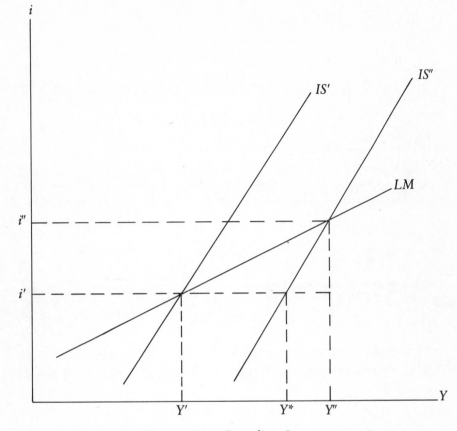

Figure 2–9. Negative Transactions Crowding Out

The *IS* curve is shifted rightwards from *IS'* to *IS"*, and the economy moves towards a new equilibrium at real GNP level *Y"* and interest rate *i"*.

Observe now that the *IS* curve shifts laterally (that is, rightwards) by the distance

$$\Delta Y_1 = Y^* - Y' \qquad (2.95)$$

However, the final total increase in the GNP level is given by the even greater distance

$$\Delta Y_2 = Y" - Y' \qquad (2.96)$$

In terms of the GNP level, a negative transactions crowding out occurs; this negative crowding out effect is described by the magnitude

$$\Delta Y_2 - \Delta Y_1 = Y^* - Y'' < 0 \tag{2.97}$$

Moreover, a similar set of results could also have been derived in the case of the open economy.

The reason underlying this negative crowding out effect is really quite simple. In particular, as the interest rate is pushed upwards as a consequence of the expansionary fiscal action, the levels of consumption and investment are raised, thereby enhancing the effect of the government spending increase, rather than offsetting it, as in the case of standard transactions crowding out. As opposed to standard (simple) transactions crowding out, where higher interest rates reduced consumption and investment and thereby reduced the efficacy of the fiscal policy, the present case generates an expansion in the GNP level that is actually greater than the simple spendings multiplier (see, for example, equation 2.47).

Mathematically, this set of conclusions can be represented quite easily. In the simple, closed economy illustrated in figure 2–9, the government spending multiplier corresponding to the case of negative transactions crowding out (that is, distance $Y'' - Y'$) is given by

$$\frac{dY}{dG} = \frac{Md_i}{(1 - C_Y - I_Y)Md_i + (C_i + I_i)Md_Y} = K^* > 0 \tag{2.98}$$

Meanwhile, the multiplier corresponding to the simple rightward shifting of the *IS* curve is given by

$$\frac{dY}{dG} = \frac{1}{(1 - C_Y - I_Y)} = K^{**} > 0 \tag{2.99}$$

The multiplier shown in equation 2.99 also can be interpreted as corresponding to zero crowding out, as in the crude Keynesian system. Finally, the multiplier corresponding to standard transactions crowding out, under the condition that $(C_i + I_i) < 0$, is given by

$$\frac{dY}{dG} = \frac{Md_i}{(1 - C_Y - I_Y)Md_i + (C_i + I_i)Md_Y} = K^{***} > 0 \tag{2.100}$$

Given that in the case of K^*, $(C_i + I_i) > 0$, whereas in the case of K^{***}, $(C_i + I_i) < 0$, it logically follows that

$$K^* > K^{**} > K^{***} > 0 \tag{2.101}$$

Thus, it follows that, in the circumstance where $(C_i + I_i) > 0$, as per Weber (1970 and 1975), Yarrow (1975), and Izenson (1983), negative transactions crowding out is presumably experienced. Moreover, the same basic conclusion can be shown to apply to the open economy in this case.

Summary

This chapter has surveyed and/or presented a number of theories of crowding out. The first case considered was the crude Classical case. The *crude Classical case of crowding out* implies a demand for money function which is completely interest inelastic. The result, in terms of an *IS - LM* analytical framework, is a completely vertical *LM* curve. The effect of a debt-financed increase in the level of government expenditures is a shift in the *IS* curve to the right. The equilibrium interest rate rises, but the level of income and the income velocity of circulation remain unchanged. In this case, the increase in the interest rate results in a reduction in private investment spending and in private consumption spending, which precisely offsets the increase in government expenditures. Crowding out is then complete.

By contrast, the crude Keynesian system was characterized by a completely vertical *IS* curve and a positively sloped *LM* curve. Within this context, zero crowding out was generated. However, as illustrated in several instances, it is entirely possible to "experience" crowding out without a vertical *LM* curve. Even in Keynes (1936, p. 120), there are passages which imply crowding out; as shown in figure 2–3, an increase in the level of government expenditures may result in crowding out by eroding confidence and resulting thusly in an increase in liquidity preference and a decrease in the marginal efficiency of capital.

Transactions crowding out was illustrated in figure 2–4. It was shown that, even with a positively sloped *LM* curve (and with the *IS* curve negatively sloped), partial crowding out would occur as rising interest rates discouraged private sector spending. Transactions crowding out is perhaps the best known of the crowding out hypotheses. Indeed, transactions crowding out is discussed in most macroeconomics textbooks.

The theory of *ultrarationality* formulated by David and Scadding (1974) implies complete crowding out. For example, if households view the government sector as an extension of themselves, an increase in government spending displaces an equal amount of private investment expenditures since households would view private investment and public investment as alternative ways of achieving an increased flow of future consumption benefits. The end result of the fiscal action, then, is a zero net change in the real GNP level; the complete crowding out is characterized simply by a reallocation of the real GNP from the private sector per se to the government sector per se.

This reallocation of GNP from the private sector to the public sector resembles somewhat the workings of the crude Classical system in figure 2–1.

As shown in figure 2–6, *financial crowding out,* which is most often associated with Friedman (1970 and 1971), implies complete crowding out. In one case, this is because the deficit, if financed by bond sales to the public, allegedly absorbs savings that would have been funneled to firms for purposes of private investment. As a result, in this case, increased government spending tends to be offset by an equally decreased private investment level.

A further possible explanation of crowding out is provided by *portfolio crowding out and real net wealth effects.* Here, a bond-financed (through sales to the public) increase in government expenditures results in an increase in household liquid wealth. Although this increase in liquid wealth may result in an increase in private consumption spending, it may also result in an increase in the aggregate demand for money. These wealth effects tend to shift both the *LM* and *IS* curves, as demonstrated in figure 2–7. The net effect of these factors, together with interest-sensitive investment and consumption functions, may lead to partial crowding out.

Klein (1972) has offered a hypothesis referred to as *portfolio substitution crowding out.* Klein argues that new government bond issues, because of their substitutability for commodities and money, shift the *IS* and *LM* curves and may thusly cause partial crowding out. Klein also includes wealth effects in his model and ensuing analysis.

Based upon the findings in Weber (1970 and 1975), Yarrow (1975), and Izenson (1983), a model in which aggregate consumption spending and aggregate investment spending are both directly related to the interest rate can be constructed. Within this model, it can be shown that a negative transactions crowding out effect conceivably could occur (and without jeopardizing the stability of the system). That is, with an expansionary fiscal action (such as $\Delta G > 0$), rising interest rates lead to increased (rather than decreased) consumption and investment and hence generate a net *negative transactions crowding out* effect (dY/dG rises as a result of $\partial I/\partial i > 0$ and $\partial C/\partial i > 0$). Of course, whether and to what degree one accepts the empirical findings that $\partial C/\partial i > 0$ and $\partial I/\partial i > 0$ is another matter entirely.

Additional Observations

In closing this chapter, it is appropriate to make a number of additional observations. To some extent, these observations may be helpful to the reader in the process of evaluation, acceptance, or rejection of any or any part of the theories of crowding out provided in this chapter.

To begin with, the survey provided here of theories of crowding out covers perhaps the better known parts of the literature. Nevertheless, this does not mean that other plausible, realistic, reasonable, or important theories of crowding out do not exist. The interested reader is referred, for additional insights into crowding out, to the contributions by Blinder and Solow (1973), Buiter (1977), Christ (1968), Eisner and Pieper (1984), Meyer (1975), Reid (1985), and Steindl (1971), among others. Moreover, this survey has not examined all of the major criticisms and/or extensions of the crowding out hypotheses examined here. For example, Smith (1939) and Cebula (1973) have both extended the analysis by Keynes (1936, p. 120) outlined in figure 2–3. Consider also the recent study by Reid (1985). Reid is concerned with the impact of deficit financing upon aggregate consumption within the context of the "permanent income hypothesis" of Milton Friedman (1957). Reid (1985, pp. 475–76) argues that if aggregate consumption "behaves in a manner consistent with the permanent income hypothesis, then statistical analysis must be careful to distinguish between permanent and transitory income flows." Using "cycle-averaged" data, Reid (1985, p. 486) finds that "permanent deficit flows exert considerable influence upon private consumption decisions." There also have been a number of criticisms of Friedman's hypothesis of financial crowding out. For instance, Van Cott and Santoni (1974) have challenged the basic tenets and conclusions of Friedman's analysis; moreover, these authors have done so rather convincingly.

Second, it has sometimes been argued that the degree of crowding out may be increased by the impact of debt-financed government spending increases that push upwards on interest rates and therefore on the value of the dollar in international currency markets. As interest rates in the United States are allegedly being pushed upwards as a result of a deficit-financed fiscal action, foreign demand for dollars rises as foreign investors seek to exchange their currency for ours in order to make financial investments in the United States. If foreign demand for dollars rises as a result of bond-financed fiscal actions elevating rates of interest in this country, then the value of the dollar may increase. If this occurs, then U.S. exports would likely decline, and U.S. imports would likely increase.[9] These effects, among other things, would tend to shift the *IS* curve downwards and to the left. In turn, the real GNP level would tend to be reduced from what it otherwise might have been, and the crowding out may then be increased above what it might otherwise have been.

Next, the analysis of crowding out provided in this chapter has stressed a number of possible crowding out causes. In the interest of simplicity, an analysis of the potential economic impacts of a changing aggregate price level has not been included. In the simpler models, such as those omitting the real wealth effect, the effect of an expansionary, bond-financed fiscal action might be to elevate the aggregate price level.[10] As a result, the *LM* curve would tend to be shifted leftwards, due to a reduced real money supply. In turn, this would in most (but not all) cases presumably result in a lower equilibrium real GNP level and hence in a greater degree of crowding out.[11] In models including a real wealth effect, the elevated aggregate price level would also act to reduce real wealth and hence to shift the *IS* curve leftwards; consequently, the equilibrium real GNP level in such cases would tend to be even further reduced.[12] And, if real wealth also were included in the money demand function, as Patinkin (1965) and others maintain, a higher price level additionally would tend to shift the *LM* curve by lowering real balances and hence real money demand.

Refer now to figure 2–10, which illustrates the impact of price-level changes upon the degree of crowding out by reconsidering the simple case of transactions crowding out. In figure 2–10, *LM**, *IS**, and *IS*** are rep-

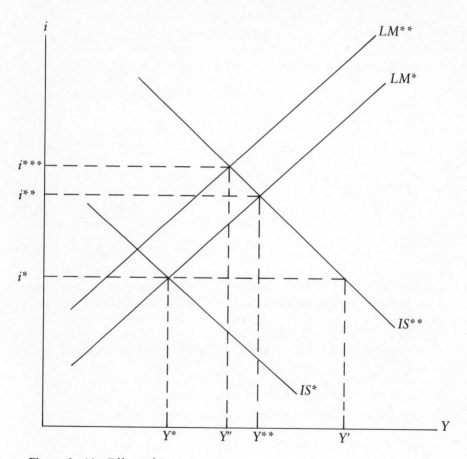

Figure 2–10. Effect of Price Increase

licated from figure 2–4; furthermore, interest rates i^* and i^{**} and real GNP levels Y^*, Y^{**}, and Y' from figure 2–4 have also been replicated. Transactions crowding out, before allowing for changes in the aggregate price level, is given by

$$Y' - Y^{**} \tag{2.102}$$

However, as a result of the aggregate price level increase resulting from the bond-financed, expansionary fiscal action, the LM curve shifts leftwards, from LM^* to LM^{**}. Transactions crowding out now rises to the amount

$$Y' - Y'' \tag{2.103}$$

Thus, while transactions crowding out is still only partial, the degree of crowding out is now greater than was the case before the aggregate price level increased, since

$$(Y' - Y'') > (Y' - Y^{**}) \tag{2.104}$$

Clearly, as the price level rose and shifted the LM curve upwards, still higher interest rates were generated. These higher interest rates in turn further diminished private sector spending and thusly increased the degree of crowding out, in this case by the amount:

$$(Y' - Y'') - (Y' - Y^{**}) = Y^{**} - Y'' > 0 \tag{2.105}$$

The positive sign shown in equation 2.105 indicates an increased degree of crowding out resulting from the effect of the aggregate price level increase on the real money supply.

Finally, there is the fact that the reader may find the plausibility or reasonableness of some crowding out theories more compelling than others.[13] As a result, the reader may wish to simply combine certain aspects of one crowding out theory with selected aspects of others.

For example, as already noted, Weber (1970 and 1975) has found aggregate consumption to be an increasing function of the interest rate:

$$C_i > 0 \tag{2.106}$$

Meanwhile, the usual (conventional) assumption regarding the relationships between aggregate investment and the interest rate is given by

$$I_i < 0 \tag{2.107}$$

Combining equations 2.106 and 2.107 yields

$$(C_i + I_i) \gtreqless 0 \text{ as } |C_i| \gtreqless |I_i| \qquad (2.108)$$

If the following is the case:

$$|C_i| = |I_i|, \qquad (2.109)$$

then it follows that the *IS* curve is perfectly vertical.

Alternatively, the findings by Yarrow (1975) and Izenson (1983), among others, are that aggregate investment is (or may be) an increasing function of the interest rate:

$$I_i > 0 \qquad (2.110)$$

Meanwhile, the conventional assumption as to the impact of interest rates upon aggregate consumption is given by

$$C_i < 0 \qquad (2.111)$$

Clearly, it follows, given equations 2.110 and 2.111, that

$$(I_i + C_i) \gtreqless 0 \text{ as } |I_i| \gtreqless |C_i| \qquad (2.112)$$

From equation 2.112, it is apparent that if

$$|I_i| = |C_i|, \qquad (2.113)$$

then the *IS* curve is perfectly vertical.

Refer now to figure 2–11, where the perfectly vertical *IS* curve *IS'* is consistent with either equation 2.109 or 2.113. If government spending rises by ΔG and ΔG is financed by bond sales to the public, the *IS* curve will shift rightwards by the full spendings multiplier (see, for example, equation 2.99) to, say, *IS''*. Obviously, as in the visually similar although behaviorally different crude Keynesian case, there will be zero crowding out under these circumstances:

$$\frac{dY}{dG} = \frac{Md_i}{(1 - C_Y - I_Y)Md_i + (C_i + I_i)Md_Y} = \frac{1}{(1 - C_Y - I_Y)} \qquad (2.114)$$

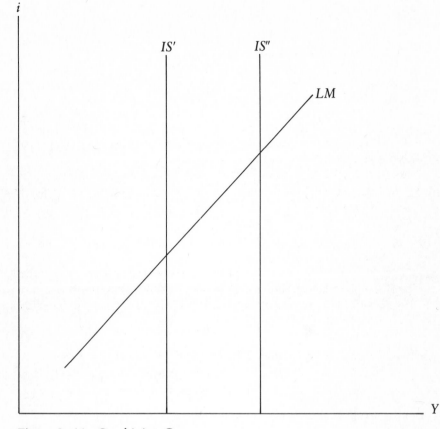

Figure 2–11. Combining Cases

This is because the term $(C_i + I_i)$ equals zero. Clearly, other possible combinations of equations 2.106 and 2.107 or equations 2.110 and 2.111 can be considered; furthermore, in each such case, different degrees of, say, transactions crowding out (or of negative transactions crowding out) can obviously be expected.

In any event, it should be stressed once again that crowding out need not be an absolute phenomenon. That is, crowding out can be either complete or partial and still be crowding out. The necessary condition, for all practical purposes, for crowding out to occur is only that dY/dG be reduced. It need not be reduced to zero, however. Moreover, dY/dG certainly need not become negative, a condition which may have important implications for system stability.[14]

Notes

1. The treatment shown in figure 2–3 is similar to that in Carlson and Spencer (1975, 6). See also the detailed treatment in Cebula (1973).

2. The possibility that $\Delta Y > 0$ is found in Carlson and Spencer (1975, 6).

3. The insightful remarks by Keynes (1936, p. 119) would seem to hint at transactions crowding out.

4. *Denison's Law* (see Denison [1958]) concerns the observed stability in the United States over time of the ratio of gross private savings to the GNP level. David and Scadding (1974) attempt to explain Denison's Law with the ultrarationality hypothesis.

5. See, for example, the observations by Hoelscher (1983, 320).

6. It is assumed that the bonds in question have not been monetized by the Federal Reserve (FED). Monetizing the deficit refers to FED purchases from the Treasury of newly issued bonds. See related paper by Baumol and Blinder (1985, pp. 293–95).

7. See, for example, figure 2–5, which illustrates ultrarationality, or figure 2–1, which illustrates crude Classical crowding out.

8. Silber (1970), Blinder and Solow (1973), and Infante and Stein (1976) have all found that bond-financed fiscal policy in the presence of wealth effects has an ambiguous impact upon the GNP level when the *IS* curve is negatively sloped. The reader may also find the paper by Hwang and Yu (1984) of relevance here.

9. Naturally, the structure of the economy is of the form:

$$Y = C + I + G + X - R,$$

where, among other things, X is a decreasing function of the value of the dollar (ceteris paribus) and R is an increasing function of the value of the dollar (ceteris paribus).

10. Of course, such an impact (upon the aggregate price level) is not always to be expected. Consider, for example, the case of the crude Classical system.

11. One exception to this outcome would be the crude Keynesian system, which is characterized by a perfectly vertical *IS* curve since $C_i = I_i = 0$.

12. In open economies, a rise in the domestic price level would, ceteris paribus, tend to lower exports and raise imports, thereby shifting the *IS* curve leftwards and implying an increased degree of crowding out if the price level increase resulted from an expansionary fiscal action.

13. Of course, the reader may feel that none of the crowding out hypotheses are appealing or valid.

14. Related to the issues of stability, crowding out, and negative multipliers, see Blinder and Solow (1973). In a different context, see also Cebula (1976, 1980); Hwang and Yu (1984); and Wang (1980).

References

Abrams, B.A. and Schmitz, M.D. 1978. "The 'Crowding Out' Effect of Government Transfers on Private Charitable Contributions." *Public Choice* 33:29–39.

Anderson, C.L. and Jordan J.L. 1968. "Monetary and Fiscal Actions: A Test of Their Relative Importance in Economic Stabilization." *Federal Reserve Bank of St. Louis Review* November: 11–24.

Arestis, P. 1979. "The 'Crowding Out' of Private Expenditures by Fiscal Actions: An Empirical Investigation." *Public Finance/Finances Publiques* 34:19–41.

Baumol, W.J. and Blinder, A.S. 1985. *Economics*. New York: Harcourt, Brace, and Jovanovich.

Batten, D.S. and Thornton, D.L. 1985. "The Anderson-Jordan Equation Revisited." *Journal of Macroeconomics* 7:419–32.

Blinder, A.S. and Solow, R.M. 1973. "Does Fiscal Policy Matter?" *Journal of Public Economics* 2:318–37.

Buiter, W.H. 1977. "Crowding Out and the Effectiveness of Fiscal Policy." *Journal of Public Economics* 7:309–28.

Carlson, K.M. and Spencer, R.W. 1975. "Crowding Out and Its Critics." *Federal Reserve Bank of St. Louis Review* December: 1–19.

Cebula, R.J. 1973. "Deficit Spending, Expectations, and Fiscal Policy Effectiveness." *Public Finance/Finances Publiques* 28:362–70.

———. 1976. "A Brief Note on Economic Policy Effectiveness." *Southern Economic Journal* 43:1174–76.

———. 1980. "IS–LM Stability and Economic Policy Effectiveness: Further Observations." *Journal of Macroeconomics* 2:181–84.

Cebula, R.J., Carlos, C., and Koch, J.M. 1981. "The 'Crowding Out' Effect of Federal Government Outlay Decisions: An Empirical Note." *Public Choice* 36:329–36.

Christ, C.F. 1968. "A Simple Macroeconomic Model with a Government Budget Restraint." *Journal of Political Economy* 76:53–67.

David, P.A. and Scadding, J.L. 1974. "Private Savings: Ultrarationality, Aggregation, and Denison's Law." *Journal of Political Economy* 82:225–49.

Denison, E.F. 1958. "A Note on Private Saving." *Review of Economics and Statistics* 40:261–67.

Dwyer, G.F. 1982. "Inflation and Government Deficits." *Economic Inquiry* 20:315–29.

Eisner, R. and Pieper, P.J. 1984. "A New View of the Federal Debt and Budget Deficit." *American Economic Review* 74:11–29.

Evans, P. 1985. "Do Large Deficits Produce High Interest Rates?" *American Economic Review* 75:68–87.

Friedman, M. 1957. *A Theory of the Consumption Function*. Princeton, New Jersey: Princeton University Press.

———. 1970. "A Theoretical Framework for Monetary Analysis." *Journal of Political Economy* 78:193–238.

———. 1971. "A Monetary Theory of Nominal Income." *Journal of Political Economy* 79:323–37.

Hoelscher, G.P. 1983. "Federal Borrowing and Short-Term Interest Rates." *Southern Economic Journal* 50:319–33.

Hwang, B.K. and Yu, E.S. 1984. "Wealth Effects, IS-LM Stability and the Efficacy of Economic Policies." *Journal of Macroeconomics* 6:229–34.

Infante, E.F. and Stein, J.L. 1976. "Does Fiscal Policy Matter?" *Journal of Monetary Economics* 2:473–500.

Izenson, M.S. 1983. "A Brief Note on the Relationship between Investment and the Interest Rate in the United States." *Economic Notes* 12:135–38.

Keran, M.W. 1970. "Monetary and Fiscal Influences on Economic Activity: The Foreign Experience." *Federal Reserve Bank of St. Louis Review* February: 16–28.

———. 1969. "Monetary and Fiscal Influences on Economic Activity—The Historical Evidence." *Federal Reserve Bank of St. Louis Review* November: 5–24.

Keynes, J.M., 1936. *The General Theory of Employment, Interest and Money.* New York: Harcourt, Brace and Company.

Klein, J.J. 1972. "More on the Analysis of Fiscal Policy and Bond Financing." *Economic Notes* 1:50–60.

Meyer, L.H. 1975. "The Balance Sheet of Identity, the Government Financing Constraint, and the Crowding Out Effect." *Journal of Monetary Economics* 4:65–78.

Meyer, P.A. 1983. "Money Multipliers and the Slopes of IS-LM." *Southern Economic Journal* 49:226–29.

Modigliani, F. "Liquidity Preference and the Theory of Interest and Money." *Econometrica.* 12:(January 1944) 45–88.

Musgrave, R. 1959. *The Theory of Public Finance,* New York: McGraw-Hill.

Patinkin, D. 1948. "Price Flexibility and Full Employment." *American Economic Review.* 38:543–64.

———. 1965. *Money, Interest, and Prices.* 2d ed. New York: Harper and Row.

Reid, B. 1985. "Aggregate Consumption and Deficit Financing: An Attempt to Separate Permanent from Transitory Effects." *Economic Inquiry* 23:475–86.

Silber, W.L. 1970. "Fiscal Policy in IS-LM Analysis: A Correction." *Journal of Money, Credit and Banking.* 2:461–73.

Smith, D.T. 1939. "Is Deficit Spending Practical?" *Harvard Business Review* 45:36–42.

Steindl, F.G. 1971. "A Simple Macroeconomic Model with a Government Budget Restraint: A Comment." *Journal of Political Economy* 79:675–79.

Sullivan, B.P. 1976. "Crowding Out Estimated from Large-Scale Econometric Model." *Federal Reserve Bank of Dallas, Business Review* June: 1–7.

Van Cott, T.N. and Santoni, G. 1974. "Friedman versus Tobin: A Comment." *Journal of Political Economy* 82:883–85.

Wang, L.F.S. 1980. "IS-LM Stability and Economic Policy Effectiveness: A Note." *Journal of Macroeconomics,* 2:175–79.

Weber, W.E. 1970. "The Effect of Interest Rates on Aggregate Consumption." *American Economic Review* 60:591–600.

———. 1975. "Interest Rates, Inflation, and Consumer Expenditures." *American Economic Review* 65:843–58.

Whitmore, H.W. 1980. "Unbalanced Government Budgets, Private Asset Holdings, and the Traditional Comparative Statics Multipliers." *Journal of Macroeconomics* 2:129–57.

Yarrow, G.K. 1975. "Growth Maximization and the Firm's Investment Function." *Southern Economic Journal* 41:580–92.

Zahn, F. 1978. "A Flow of Funds Analysis of Crowding Out." *Southern Economic Journal* 45:195–206.

3

An Empirical Analysis of Crowding Out: The Search for a Transmission Mechanism

As shown in the preceding chapter, crowding out can, in theory, assume a large variety of different forms, including classical crowding out, simple transactions crowding out, ultrarationality, financial crowding out, portfolio crowding out, and portfolio substitution crowding out. Of these forms, transactions crowding out is probably the best known. Figure 2–4 illustrated the transactions crowding out impact of a rise in government spending financed entirely by treasury bond sales to the private sector of the economy. In figure 2–4, the *IS* curve shifted upwards from *IS** to *IS***, and the economy moved from its original *IS–LM* equilibrium at (Y^*, i^*) to a new *IS-LM* equilibrium at (Y^{**}, i^{**}). In figure 2–4, transactions crowding out is indicated by the distance from Y^{**} to Y'. Note that a key trait of this form of crowding out is a net rise in the rate of interest. Other forms of crowding out, including portfolio crowding out and portfolio substitution crowding out, are also characterized by rising interest rate levels.

Numerous empirical studies investigating the possible existence of crowding out and the degree of crowding out have appeared during recent years (see, for example, Abrams and Schmitz [1978], Anderson and Jordan [1968], Arestis [1979], Cebula [1985], Keran [1969 and 1970], Sullivan [1976], and Zahn [1978]). Although these studies attempt to measure the degree of crowding out per se, they do not attempt to identify or verify the existence of the actual mechanism by which crowding out may be transmitted to the economy at large. For instance, the studies cited above do not attempt to verify whether a federal budget deficit exercises any impact over interest rates, as would be the case for transactions crowding out, portfolio crowding out, and portfolio substitution crowding out, to name just a few relevant crowding out forms. As indicated in the following section of this chapter, however, a recent literature has appeared which does attempt to address this very issue.

The Literature on Federal Borrowing and Interest Rates

A number of recent studies have focused upon the possible impact of federal government borrowings upon interest rates. For instance, Hoelscher (1983, p. 319) empirically examines "the effects of federal government borrowing on short-term interest rates." Hoelscher's analysis is based upon regressions that test whether the level of federal borrowing is a statistically significant determinant of the three-month Treasury bill rate. Hoelscher (1983, p. 319) obtains extremely low *t*-values on the relevant coefficients and hence concludes that "Federal borrowing is a relatively unimportant . . . determinant of short-term rates." Accordingly, Hoelscher (1983, p. 332) concludes that "to the extent that private expenditures are sensitive only to short-term rates, then Federal borrowing does not have financial crowding out effects." Hoelscher comes to this conclusion despite his confusion over the distinction between "transactions crowding out" and "financial crowding out" (1983, p. 320). Makin (1983) has also examined the impact of federal government borrowing on the three-month Treasury bill rate. Like Hoelscher, Makin (1983, p. 381) finds federal borrowing has very little (if any) impact upon the three-month Treasury bill rate: "Based on equation 6(b) a \$100 billion deficit would elevate short-term interest rates by only 10 basis points." Accordingly, Makin (1983, p. 382) concludes that "Overall, the results reported here regarding the possible significance of 'crowding out' can only be judged as 'mixed to weak'."

Results very similar to those in Hoelscher and Makin have also been obtained by Motley (1983) and, in the empirical analysis of the three-month Treasury bill rate, by Mascaro and Meltzer (1983). Interestingly, Mascaro and Meltzer also find the interest rate yield on ten-year Treasury notes to be unaffected by federal budget deficits.

On the other hand, a recent comment on the Hoelscher paper by Barth, Iden, and Russek (1985, p. 556) finds that, after adjusting the federal deficit for the effects of cyclical activity, the resulting "structural deficit" has a "positive and highly significant impact on the 3 month Treasury bill rate." Yet another very recent study, by Evans (1985), examines the impact of federal deficits upon the three-month Treasury bill rate (and selected other interest rates) for four separate time periods in U.S. history (the Civil War period, World War I, World War II, and the period from October 1979 to December 1983). Evans' analysis may be marred by multicolinearity problems between two of his so-called exogenous variables, namely "*GR*" (the ratio of real federal spending to trend real national income) and "*DR*" (the ratio of the real federal deficit to trend real national income). This is because a pattern of both federal spending growth and federal deficit growth is characteristic of each of the four periods of Evans' investigation. Nevertheless, like the earlier studies by Hoelscher (1983), Makin (1983), Motley (1983), and Mascaro and Meltzer (1983), Evans (1985, p. 68) finds "no evidence for a positive association between deficits and interest rates."

All of these studies are concerned ultimately with the possible crowding out that can result from federal deficits (borrowing). Moreover, in conjunction with this concern over crowding out, most of these studies basically stress the impact of deficits upon the three-month Treasury bill rate. Exceptions include the paper by Mascaro and Meltzer (1983), which also examines the rate on ten-year Treasury notes but finds this longer term rate to be unaffected by federal deficits, and the paper by Evans (1985), which also considers selected alternative interest rate measures, each of which is found to be apparently insensitive to federal deficits. There is a potential problem with this entire procedure of stressing the three-month Treasury bill rate, however. In particular, firms (and/or households) may make investment (and/or other outlay) decisions predicated, among other factors, upon longer term interest rates, *not* simply and solely short-term interest rates. As Hoelscher (1983, p. 332) himself concedes, "If private expenditures are also sensitive to medium or long-term rates, then . . . crowding out is possible." Indeed, it might have been highly desirable for previous studies such as Hoelscher's (1983) to have examined not only the three-month Treasury bill rate but also longer term rates (such as the rate on Treasury notes or bonds).

In addition, and more importantly, a feature common to nearly all of this literature (see Barth, Iden, and Russek [1985] for an exception) is the measurement of the federal deficit as the mere excess of federal outlays over receipts. In other words, there exists a widespread practice of failing to control for the effects of the business cycle by removing the cyclical component of the deficit from the total deficit to yield the so-called structural deficit. Later on in this chapter, it will be argued that an examination of the impact of the structural deficit may be far more insightful and useful than an investigation involving the total deficit per se.

The purpose of the remainder of this chapter is to examine the interest rate impact of federal budget deficits. First, a simple theoretical model is developed. Then, an empirical analysis is provided. The latter analysis argues that: (1) It may be useful to examine the possible impact of federal deficits not only upon the three-month Treasury bill rate but also upon the longer term rate such as that on ten-year Treasury notes; and (2) it may be far more insightful and useful to examine the impact of the structural deficit than the total deficit per se.

A Simple Model

As illustrated in chapter 2, the crowding out phenomenon is perhaps most frequently analyzed and depicted within an *IS-LM* framework. Consider, for example, the following simple model:

$$Y = C + I + G + X - R \tag{3.1}$$

$$C = \bar{a} + C(Yd, i) \tag{3.2}$$

$$I = \bar{I} + I(Y, i) \tag{3.3}$$

$$G = \overline{G} \tag{3.4}$$

$$T = \overline{T} \tag{3.5}$$

$$X = \overline{X} \tag{3.6}$$

$$R = \overline{R} + R(Y) \tag{3.7}$$

$$M = Md \tag{3.8}$$

$$M = \overline{M} \tag{3.9}$$

$$Md = \overline{Z} + Md(Y, i), \tag{3.10}$$

where Y is aggregate income; C is aggregate consumption; I is aggregate investment; G is aggregate government spending; X is aggregate exports; R is aggregate imports; Yd is aggregate disposable income; i is the interest rate; $\bar{a}$ is autonomous consumption; $\bar{I}$ is autonomous investment; $\overline{G}$ is exogenous government spending; $\overline{T}$ is exogenous tax collections; $\overline{X}$ is exogenous exports; $\overline{R}$ is autonomous imports; M is the money stock; Md is aggregate money demand; $\overline{M}$ is the exogenous money stock; and $\overline{Z}$ is exogenous money demand. Following chapter 2, subscripts are used to indicate partial (or total) differentiation. The behavior within this system is then described by

$$1 > C_{Yd} > 0 \tag{3.11}$$

$$C_i < 0 \tag{3.12}$$

$$1 > I_y > 0 \tag{3.13}$$

$$I_i < 0 \tag{3.14}$$

$$1 > R_y > 0 \qquad (3.15)$$

$$Md_y > 0 \qquad (3.16)$$

$$Md_i < 0 \qquad (3.17)$$

Given $T = \overline{T}$, it follows that

$$C_{Yd} = C_y \qquad (3.18)$$

Accordingly, the slope of the *IS* curve in this system is given by

$$\frac{1 - C_y - I_y + R_y}{C_i + I_i} < 0 \qquad (3.19)$$

The slope of the *LM* curve in this system is given by

$$\frac{-Md_y}{Md_i} > 0 \qquad (3.20)$$

Using the simple stability analysis outlined in chapter 2, it can be easily shown that a stable *IS-LM* equilibrium requires that

$$\frac{1 - C_y - I_y + R_y}{C_i + I_i} < \frac{-Md_y}{Md_i} \qquad (3.21)$$

The preceding system is indeed a very simple one. For example, notice the omission of any form of wealth effect or a variable price level. Nevertheless, it is a useful point of departure for further analysis. As shown in chapter 2, the equilibrium rate of interest is determined at the intersection of the *IS* and *LM* curves. Starting at an *IS-LM* equilibrium, a rise in government spending financed entirely by Treasury borrowings from the private sector will shift the *IS* curve upwards and result in a rise in the rate of interest. This is demonstrated by

$$\frac{\partial i}{\partial G} = \frac{-Md_y}{(1 - C_y - I_y + R_y)Md_i + (C_i + I_i)Md_y} > 0 \qquad (3.22)$$

Thus, as shown in figure 2–4, a deficit-financed rise in government spending acts, among other things, to raise the rate of interest.[1] Indeed, it is just this sort of interest rate increase that is associated with, say, transactions crowding out. Naturally, a tax cut, financed by Treasury borrowings from the private sector, would also shift up the *IS* curve and push the rate of interest upwards.

Starting once again in *IS-LM* equilibrium, a rise in the exogenous money stock (that is, an expansionary monetary policy) shifts the *LM* curve downwards. A new equilibrium is then established at a lower rate of interest and a higher level of aggregate income. The impact of this policy on the rate of interest is shown by[2]

$$\frac{\partial i}{\partial M} = \frac{(1 - C_y - I_y + R_y)}{(1 - C_y - I_y + R_y)Md_i + (C_i + I_i)Md_y} < 0 \qquad (3.23)$$

Thus, in the simple model shown in equations 3.1 through 3.21, deficits are associated with higher interest rates, and monetary expansion is associated with lower interest rates. Naturally, as the model is expanded to include additional behavioral traits and variables, the mathematics will become more involved. Nevertheless, as Hoelscher (1983, p. 321) correctly observes, it has become commonplace for most authors and researchers to assume that "interest rates will rise with . . . deficit spending." To a large degree, the empirical section that follows will address the validity of this assumption. In this empirical investigation, the analysis will attempt to control for the potential impacts of monetary expansion (which presumably acts to reduce interest rate levels) and other factors as well.

Empirical Analysis

As illustrated in the preceding section of this chapter (and in chapter 2 as well), the conventional *IS-LM* paradigm indicates that (ceteris paribus): A deficit-financed government spending increase leads to a higher rate of interest, and an expansionary monetary policy leads to a lower rate of interest. Of course, such conclusions merely follow from the paradigm and require empirical verification. As a point of departure for such an empirical verification, consider the following simple model:

$$i = i(DEF, M) \qquad (3.24)$$

where *i* is the rate of interest, *DEF* is the size of the deficit, and *M* is the size of the money stock. Naturally, we need not depend upon the *IS-LM* paradigm to infer the possible relationships suggested by equation 3.24. On the one hand, it would be a simple matter to derive such inferences from a loanable funds model. On the other hand, as exemplified in the studies by Hoelscher (1983), Makin (1983), Motley (1983), Mascaro and Meltzer

(1983), Barth, Iden, and Russek (1985), and Evans (1985), there exists a considerable empirical/theoretical literature that investigates the impact of the deficit upon the interest rate. Moreover, in the process of investigation of this deficit–interest rate relationship, a number of these studies, including those by Mascaro and Meltzer (1983), Makin (1983), Motley (1983), and Evans (1985), allow for the interest rate impact of monetary growth or the magnitude of the money supply.

Perhaps the first issue that should be addressed is that of defining and measuring the deficit. Although there are notable exceptions (such as Barth, Iden, and Russek [1985]), it is commonplace in this literature to measure the deficit as simply the difference between aggregate federal outlays and receipts. That is, most of the literature fails to adjust the aggregate federal budget deficit for the effects of the business cycle.

It might be useful here to make a few observations regarding the relationship between the deficit and the business cycle. Consider, for instance, the traits of an economic downturn. As real GNP declines, government tax collections decline and government transfer payments to the private sector increase. Thus, the total federal deficit increases, and federal credit demands increase. However, concurrent with the *increased* credit demands of the Treasury will be *decreased* credit demands on the part of the private sector of the economy because the downturn in real GNP will elicit diminished real consumption and/or diminished real investment. Thus, the cyclical component of the federal deficit is accompanied by a cyclical decline in private sector spending (and credit demand). As a result, the increased credit demands of the Treasury to finance its "cyclical deficit" are presumably going to be significantly offset (perhaps entirely offset, or more) by diminished private sector credit demands during the same downturn. As Barth, Iden, and Russek (1985, p. 555) observe, the contracyclical "movement of federal deficits and the procyclical movement of interest rates may produce a downwardly biased estimate of the effect of deficits on interest rates." Accordingly, when examining the interest rate impact of the federal deficit, it can be reasonably argued that the cyclical component of that deficit should be ignored and only the remaining, noncyclical component of the deficit—the so-called *structural deficit*—should be examined.

Stated somewhat differently, the total federal deficit moves contracyclically whereas interest rates and private sector credit demand move procyclically. Thus, for example, it presumably is not the rising deficit but rather simultaneous and more rapidly declining private sector credit demands that push interest rates downwards during an economic downturn. Accordingly, unless an empirical analysis expressly includes a variable that directly and meaningfully measures the magnitude of private sector credit demands, then it must use the structural deficit rather than the total deficit if it is to avoid a serious misspecification.

This chapter uses estimates of the structural deficit provided in the study by Holloway (1986). Holloway provides revised and updated quarterly estimates of the structural deficit for the period 1955:I through 1985:IV.[3] In addition, Holloway provides other data used in this chapter, including revised and updated quarterly estimates of trend GNP.

The next issue to address is that of choosing an interest rate measure. Most of the literature has focused upon the three-month Treasury bill rate. Although this focus may be reasonable, it might also be useful to focus upon a longer-term rate, such as the rate on ten-year Treasury notes. In other words, when private sector firms and consumers are formulating their expenditure decisions, they very plausibly may focus upon interest rates other than simply the short-term (three-month) rate. This emphasis upon both a three-month rate and a ten-year rate is found in certain other studies, such as Mascaro and Meltzer (1983).

Given the preceding observations, the following two regression equations may be hypothesized:

$$TBR_t = a_0 + a_1 STDEF_t/Y_t + a_2 M1_t/Y_t + \mu_1 \qquad (3.25)$$

$$TNR_t = b_0 + b_1 STDEF_t/Y_t + b_2 M1_t/Y_t + \mu_2, \qquad (3.26)$$

where a_0 and b_0 are constant terms; TBR_t is interest rate yield on three-month Treasury bills in quarter t; TNR_t is interest rate yield on ten-year Treasury notes in quarter t; $STDEF_t/Y_t$ is ratio of the structural deficit in quarter t to trend GNP in quarter t; $M1_t/Y_t$ is ratio of the seasonally adjusted M1 measure of the money stock in quarter t to trend GNP in quarter t; and μ_1 and μ_2 are stochastic error terms. Following Evans (1985) and Hoelscher (1983, p. 324), the deficit variable is scaled (divided) by trend GNP. This procedure allows for the secular drift of aggregate income over time. Moreover, the structural deficit is divided by trend GNP because federal government deficits should be evaluated vis-à-vis the size of the economy that must finance them. Similarly, following the studies by Evans and others, the monetary variable is also divided by trend GNP.

On the basis of the *IS-LM* paradigm, it is argued that deficits act to raise the rate of interest, ceteris paribus. Accordingly, it is expected that

$$a_1, b_1 > 0 \qquad (3.27)$$

This is in effect the same basic hypothesis investigated by Hoelscher (1983), Makin (1983), Motley (1983), Evans (1985), Barth, Iden and Russek (1985), and Mascaro and Meltzer (1983). In addition, according to the conventional wisdom, it is expected that

$$a_2, b_2 < 0 \qquad (3.28)$$

In the interest of being as current as possible, the basic time period to be studied runs from 1975:I through 1985:IV. Estimating equations 3.25 and 3.26 by ordinary least squares (OLS) yields equations 3.29 and 3.30, respectively:

$$TBR_t = 0.502 + 0.357 \ STDEF_t/Y_t - 2.70 \ M1_t/Y_t,$$
$$(+2.41) \qquad\qquad (-6.72)$$
$$R^2 = 0.59, \overline{R}^2 = 0.57, DF = 41, DW = 1.78 \quad (3.29)$$

$$TNR_t = 0.470 + 0.209 \ STDEF_t/Y_t - 2.39 \ M1_t/Y_t,$$
$$(+2.40) \qquad\qquad (-11.63)$$
$$R^2 = 0.83, \overline{R}^2 = 0.82, DF = 41, DW = 1.71 \quad (3.30)$$

where terms in parentheses beneath coefficients are t-values.

In equation 3.29, both coefficients have the expected signs and are statistically significant at beyond the 0.01 level. The coefficient of determination is 0.59, so that the model explains nearly three-fifths of the variation in the three-month Treasury bill rate over the period. In equation 3.30, both coefficients have the expected signs and are statistically significant at beyond the 0.01 level. In this case, the coefficient of determination is 0.83, so that the model explains over four-fifths of the variation in the ten-year Treasury note rate over the period.

In terms of the basic objective of this chapter, the most relevant finding is that the structural deficit does in fact exercise a positive and statistically significant impact upon both the three-month Treasury bill rate and the ten-year Treasury note rate.[4] This finding is compatible with Barth, Iden, and Russek (1985) and with a somewhat related earlier study by Feldstein and Eckstein (1970). On the other hand, this finding is altogether at odds with the bulk of the literature, including Hoelscher (1983), Makin (1983), Motley (1983), Evans (1985), and Mascaro and Meltzer (1983).

It should also be noted that this positive and statistically significant impact of the deficit upon TBR_t and TNR_t is not restricted solely to the period 1975:I through 1985:IV. For instance, examining the period 1979 through 1983 considered relevant in the Evans (1985, pp. 82–85) study yields the following results:

$$TBR_t = 0.505 + 2.166 \ STDEF_t/Y_t - 2.39 \ M1_t/Y_t,$$
$$(+4.58) \qquad\qquad (-4.87)$$
$$R^2 = 0.61, \overline{R}^2 = 0.57, DF = 17, DW = 1.85 \quad (3.31)$$

$$TNR_t = 0.532 + 0.896 \ STDEF_t/Y_t - 2.72 \ M1_t/Y_t,$$
$$(+3.58) \qquad\qquad (-10.43)$$
$$R^2 = 0.84, \overline{R}^2 = 0.82, DF = 17, DW = 1.72 \quad (3.32)$$

During this time period (1979:I through 1983:IV), once again observe that the deficit variable exercises a positive and statistically significant impact upon both the three-month Treasury bill rate and the ten-year Treasury note rate.

Moreover, essentially the same basic findings are obtained for other time periods. Consider, for example, the OLS results shown below for the period 1970:I through 1979:IV:

$$TBR_t = 0.189 + \underset{(+3.25)}{1.15} \ STDEF_t/Y_t - \underset{(-4.09)}{0.599} \ M1_t/Y_t,$$

$$R^2 = 0.34, \overline{R}^2 = 0.30, DF = 37, DW = 1.86 \quad (3.33)$$

$$TNR_t = 0.154 + \underset{(+2.11)}{0.165} \ STDEF_t/Y_t - \underset{(-6.89)}{0.426} \ M1_t/Y_t,$$

$$R^2 = 0.59, \overline{R}^2 = 0.57, DF = 37, DW = 1.79 \quad (3.34)$$

Of course, it can be very reasonably argued that other factors should be integrated into the analysis. For instance, the studies by Barth, Iden, and Russek (1985), Hoelscher (1983), and Tanzi (1980) suggest the use of the unemployment rate when trying to explain the interest rate.

The regression equations now to be considered are the following:

$$TBR_t = c_0 + c_1 \ STDEF_t/Y_t + c_2 M1_t/Y_t + c_3 \ UNEMP_t + \mu_3 \quad (3.35)$$

$$TNR_t = d_0 + d_1 \ STDEF_t/Y_t + d_2 M1_t/Y_t + d_3 \ UNEMP_t + \mu_4 \quad (3.36)$$

where c_0 and d_0 are constant terms; $UNEMP_t$ is seasonally adjusted aggregate unemployment rate in quarter t; and μ_3 and μ_4 are stochastic error terms. In order to be as current as possible, return once again to the time period 1975:I through 1985:IV.

The studies by Barth, Iden, and Russek (1985), Hoelscher (1983), and Tanzi (1980) all find that higher unemployment rates tend to imply reduced private sector credit demands and hence lower interest rate levels. Accordingly, it is expected that

$$c_3, d_3 < 0 \quad (3.37)$$

The OLS estimates of equations 3.35 and 3.36 are given by equations 3.38 and 3.39, respectively:

$$TBR_t = 0.739 + 0.657 \ STDEF_t/Y_t - 3.66 \ M1_t/Y_t$$
$$\qquad\qquad (+4.55) \qquad\qquad\quad (-10.05)$$
$$- \ 1.12 \ UNEMP_t, R^2 = 0.75, \overline{R}^2 = 0.74, DF = 40, DW = 1.77$$
$$(-5.21)$$

$$(3.38)$$

$$TNR_t = 0.516 + 0.267 \ STDEF_t/Y_t - 2.58 \ M1_t/Y_t$$
$$\qquad\qquad (+2.86) \qquad\qquad\quad (-10.98)$$
$$- \ 0.216 \ UNEMP_t, R^2 = 0.84, \overline{R}^2 = 0.83, DF = 40, DW = 1.65$$
$$(-1.56)$$

$$(3.39)$$

In equations 3.38 and 3.39, all six estimated coefficients have the expected signs, and five of the six are statistically significant beyond the 0.01 level. Only the coefficient on the unemployment rate variable in equation 3.39 fails to be significant at an acceptable (that is, 0.05) level. The R^2 in equation 3.38 is 0.75, indicating that the model explains roughly three-fourths of the variation in the three-month Treasury bill rate. The R^2 in equation 3.39 is 0.84, indicating that the model explains over four-fifths of the variation in the ten-year Treasury note rate.

Given the objectives of this chapter, the most relevant findings in equations 3.38 and 3.39 are the coefficients on the deficit variable. As shown, the deficit exercises a positive and statistically significant impact upon both the three-month Treasury bill rate and the ten-year Treasury note rate. These results are consistent with the earlier estimates provided in this chapter. Thus, including the unemployment rate in the model does not alter the basic findings regarding the impact of deficits upon TBR_t and TNR_t. Other time periods, such as 1979:I through 1983:IV and 1970:I through 1979:IV yield similar results.[5] In order to save space, however, these additional estimates are not provided here.

Of course, the unemployment rate is not the only reasonable surrogate for the pace of economic activity. For example, the growth rate of real GNP would presumably be a suitable surrogate as well. Consider now the following regressions, where the growth rate of real GNP is substituted for the unemployment rate:

$$TBR_t = e_0 + e_1 \ STDEF_t/Y_t + e_2 M1_t/Y_t + e_3 \ \Delta GNP_t + \mu_5 \quad (3.40)$$

$$TNR_t = f_0 + f_1 \ STDEF_t/Y_t + f_2 M1_t/Y_t + f_3 \ \Delta GNP_t + \mu_6, \quad (3.41)$$

where e_0, f_0 are constant terms; ΔGNP_t is the percentage change in actual real GNP during quarter t; and μ_5 and μ_6 are stochastic error terms. Once again, in the interest of being as current as possible, consider the time period 1975:I through 1985:IV.

Presumably, a higher real GNP growth rate may imply a more robust growth in private sector credit demands. Accordingly, one might expect that

$$e_3, f_3 > 0 \qquad (3.42)$$

The OLS estimates of equations 3.40 and 3.41 are given by equations 3.43 and 3.44, respectively:

$$TBR_t = 0.510 + \underset{(+2.07)}{0.343} \ STDEF_t/Y_t - \underset{(-7.10)}{2.82} \ M1_t/Y_t$$
$$+ \underset{(+1.79)}{0.11} \ \Delta GNP_t, R^2 = 0.62, \overline{R}^2 = 0.59, DF = 40, DW = 1.81 \qquad (3.43)$$

$$TNR_t = 0.472 + \underset{(+2.35)}{0.206} \ STDEF_t/Y_t - \underset{(-11.53)}{2.42} \ M1_t/Y_t$$
$$+ \underset{(+0.78)}{0.02} \ \Delta GNP_t, R^2 = 0.83, \overline{R}^2 = 0.82, DF = 40, DW = 1.80 \qquad (3.44)$$

In equations 3.43 and 3.44, the coefficients on the real GNP growth variable, ΔGNP_t, while both positive, are not statistically significant at an acceptable level. Nevertheless, observe the positive and statistically significant coefficients on the deficit variable in both estimates. Thus, observe once again that deficits exercise a positive and statistically significant impact upon both the three-month Treasury bill rate and the ten-year Treasury note rate.

In terms of the variable ΔGNP_t, it may be interesting to refer briefly to the OLS estimates of equations 3.40 and 3.41 for the period 1979:I through 1983:IV. These results are provided in equations 3.45 and 3.46:

$$TBR_t = 0.553 + \underset{(+4.98)}{2.177} \ STDEF_t/Y_t - \underset{(-5.67)}{2.81} \ M1_t/Y_t$$
$$+ \underset{(+2.13)}{0.14} \ \Delta GNP_t, R^2 = 0.68, \overline{R}^2 = 0.64, DF = 16, DW = 1.82 \qquad (3.45)$$

$$TNR_t = 0.556 + \underset{(+3.82)}{0.902} \ STDEF_t/Y_t - \underset{(-10.89)}{2.92} \ M1_t/Y_t$$
$$+ \underset{(+1.89)}{0.07} \ \Delta GNP_t, R^2 = 0.86, \overline{R}^2 = 0.84, DF = 16, DW = 1.81 \qquad (3.46)$$

In these two estimates, where the coefficients on variable ΔGNP_t are positive and statistically significant at roughly the 0.05 level, all coefficients exhibit the expected signs and are statistically significant. Thus, once again, a positive and statistically significant impact of the deficit upon the levels of TBR_t and TNR_t is generated.

Naturally, other model specifications might reasonably be considered. For example, in order to allow for partial adjustment of the interest rate to changes in the explanatory variables, it may be appropriate to include a one-quarter lag of the interest rate series as a right-hand side variable. To examine such a specification, consider the following equations:

$$TBR_t = g_0 + g_1 \, STDEF_t/Y_t + g_2 M1_t/Y_t$$
$$+ g_3 \, UNEMP_t + g_4 TBR_{t-1} + \mu_7 \quad (3.47)$$

$$TNR_t = h_0 + h_1 \, STDEF_t/Y_t + h_2 M1_t/Y_t$$
$$+ h_3 \, UNEMP_t + h_4 TNR_{t-1} + \mu_8, \quad (3.48)$$

where g_0 and h_0 are constant terms and μ_7 and μ_8 are stochastic error terms. Once again, the focus is on the period 1975:I through 1985:IV.

The OLS estimates of equations 3.47 and 3.48 are given by equations 3.49 and 3.50, respectively:

$$TBR_t = 0.181 + 0.269 \, STDEF_t/Y_t - 0.77 \, M1_t/Y_t$$
$$(+2.46) \qquad\qquad (-1.95)$$
$$- 0.400 \, UNEMP_t + 0.69 \, TBR_{t-1}, \quad (3.49)$$
$$(-2.35) \qquad\qquad (+5.36)$$
$$R^2 = 0.83, \overline{R}^2 = 0.82, DF = 39, DW = 1.65$$

$$TNR_t = 0.304 + 0.175 \, STDEF_t/Y_t - 0.42 \, M1_t/Y_t$$
$$(+2.26) \qquad\qquad (-1.97)$$
$$- 0.161 \, UNEMP_t + 0.79 \, TNR_{t-1}, \quad (3.50)$$
$$(-1.38) \qquad\qquad (+14.72)$$
$$R^2 = 0.96, \overline{R}^2 = 0.95, DF = 39, DW = 1.61$$

As shown in equations 3.49 and 3.50, it can once again be observed that deficits exercise a positive and statistically significant impact upon both the three-month Treasury bill rate and the ten-year Treasury note rate.

Conclusions

Naturally, other model specifications might reasonably be considered. In point of fact, a number of such regressions have been estimated. Some of these contain a lagged version of the monetary variable. In a number of estimations, expected inflation has also been introduced. In addition, the unemployment variable and real GNP growth variable have been lagged in a variety of ways. A variety of different time periods have also been investigated, beginning with 1955:I.

The various estimations described in the preceding paragraph generate two clear patterns of relevant empirical results. First, deficits exercise a positive and statistically significant impact upon the three-month Treasury bill rate. Second, deficits exercise a positive and statistically significant impact upon the ten-year Treasury note rate. These two conclusions are consistent with all of the estimations provided in the preceding section of this chapter. Moreover, although at odds with the studies by Hoelscher (1983), Makin (1983), Motley (1983), Evans (1985), and Mascaro and Meltzer (1983), these two conclusions are consistent with studies by Barth, Iden, and Russek (1984 and 1985) and Feldstein and Eckstein (1970). For the period 1975–1985, if the structural deficit is 2.5 percent of the GNP level, then the empirical results imply that the three-month Treasury bill rate will rise by 65 to 165 basis points whereas the ten-year Treasury note rate will rise by 40 to 65 basis points. In any event, the empirical results presented in this chapter imply the actual existence of a mechanism for the transmission of crowding out. Unlike most earlier studies, then, the present study suggests a relatively greater need to come to grips with the problems of huge deficits and an enormous national debt.[6]

Notes

1. The simple government spendings (deficit) multiplier is given by:

$$\frac{\partial Y}{\partial \overline{G}} = \frac{Md_i}{(1 - C_y - I_y + R_y)Md_i + (C_i + I_i)Md_y} > 0$$

2. The simple multiplier in this instance is given by:

$$\frac{\partial Y}{\partial \overline{M}} = \frac{C_i + I_i}{(1 - C_y - I_y + R_y)Md_i + (C_i + I_i)Md_y} > 0$$

3. Regarding structural deficit data available prior to the publication of the Holloway (1986) study, the reader is referred to de Leeuw and Holloway (1982) and to the study by the U.S. Congressional Budget Office (1984, Appendix A).

4. Given the absence of any significant market segmentation, one would expect that if one of these rates is impacted then the other would likely be impacted as well.

5. It is interesting to note that the unemployment variable also is a significant determinant of TBR_t for the longer period 1970:I through 1985:IV. This fact is illustrated in the following OLS estimation for the period:

$$TBR_t = 0.375 + 0.715 \ STDEF_t/Y_t - 1.39 \ M1_t/Y_t - 0.714 \ UNEMP_t,$$
$$\quad\quad\quad (+3.14) \quad\quad\quad\quad (-8.93) \quad\quad\quad (-3.02)$$
$$R^2 = 0.60, \ \overline{R}^2 = 0.58, \ DF = 60, \ DW = 1.75.$$

6. Of course, the empirical findings in this chapter are all the more important when one considers the highly significant impact of U.S. interest rates upon the value of the U.S. dollar in international currency markets.

References

Abrams, B.A. and Schmitz, M.D. 1978. "The 'Crowding Out' Effect of Government Transfers on Private Charitable Contributions." *Public Choice* 33:29–39.

Anderson, C.L. and Jordan, J.L. 1968. "Monetary and Fiscal Actions: A Test of Their Relative Importance in Economic Stabilization." *Federal Reserve Bank of St. Louis Review* November: 11–24.

Arestis, P. 1979. " 'The Crowding Out' of Private Expenditure by Fiscal Actions: An Empirical Investigation." *Public Finance/Finances Publiques* 34:19–41.

Barth, J.R., Iden, G., and Russek, F.S. 1984. "Do Deficits Really Matter?" *Contemporary Policy Issues* 3:79–95.

———. 1985. "Federal Borrowing and Short Term Interest Rates: Comment," *Southern Economic Journal* 50:554–59.

Cebula, R.J. 1985. "Crowding Out and Fiscal Policy in the United States: A Note on the Recent Experience." *Public Finance/Finances Publiques* 40:133–36.

deLeeuw, F., and Holloway, T.M. 1982. "The High-Employment Budget: Revised Estimates and Automatic Inflation Effects." *Survey of Current Business* 62:21–33.

Evans, P. 1985. "Do Large Deficits Produce High Interest Rates?" *American Economic Review* 75:68–87.

Feldstein, M. and Eckstein, O. 1970. "The Fundamental Determinants of the Interest Rate." *Review of Economics and Statistics* 52:363–75.

Hoelscher, G. 1983. "Federal Borrowing and Short Term Interest Rates." *Southern Economic Journal* 50:319–33.

Holloway, T.M. 1986. "The Cyclically Adjusted Federal Budget and Federal Debt: Revised and Updated Estimates." *Survey of Current Business* 66:11–17.

Keran, M.W. 1969. "Monetary and Fiscal Influences on Economic Activity—The Historical Evidence." *Federal Reserve Bank of St. Louis Review* November: 5–24.

———. "Monetary and Fiscal Influences on Economic Activity: The Foreign Experience." *Federal Reserve Bank of St. Louis Review* February: 16–28.

Makin, John H. 1983. "Real Interest, Money Surprises, Anticipated Inflation and Fiscal Deficits." *Review of Economics and Statistics* 65:374–84.

Mascaro, Angelo and Meltzer, A.H. 1983. "Long- and Short-Term Interest Rates in a Risky World." *Journal of Monetary Economics* 10:485–518.

Mishkin, F.S. 1981. "The Real Interest Rate: An Empirical Investigation." *Carnegie-Rochester Conference Series on Public Policy*: 151–200.

Motley, B. 1983. "Real Interest Rates, Money, and Government Deficits." *Federal Reserve Bank of San Francisco, Economic Review* Summer: 31–45.

Sullivan, B.P. 1976. "Crowding Out Estimated from Large-Scale Econometric Model." *Federal Reserve Bank of Dallas, Business Review* June: 1–7.

Tanzi, V. 1970. "Inflationary Expectations, Economic Activity, Taxes, and Interest Rates." *American Economic Review* 70:12–21.

U.S. Congressional Budget Office. 1984. "Deficits and Interest Rates: Empirical Findings and Selected Bibliography." *The Economic Outlook*. Washington, D.C.: U.S. Government Printing Office.

Zahn, F. 1978. "A Flow of Funds Analysis of Crowding Out." *Southern Economic Journal* 45:195–206.

4
Controlling the Deficit: The Constitutional Amendment Approach

D espite the very strong empirical evidence in chapter 3, there currently exists in the literature conflicting evidence as to the impacts of federal budget deficits. The conflicting evidence involves, among other things, the following: (1) as indicated by the analysis in chapter 3, the identity of the mechanism or mechanisms through which the deficit impacts upon the economy; and (2) the extent (if any) to which negative economic consequences result from the deficit.

On the other hand, although there are still a number of dissenters, most policymakers seem to agree that something must be done to control the size of the federal budget deficit. There are a number of possible general means for dealing with the deficit, including the following: (1) tax reform; (2) tax increases; (3) cuts in defense expenditures; (4) cuts in nondefense expenditures; (5) coordinated expansionary monetary policies; and (6) a balanced-budget amendment to the U.S. Constitution. Chapter 5 will briefly address in general terms certain aspects of the issues associated with items (1), (2), (3), (4), and (5). Meanwhile, the present chapter addresses item (6), an item that has received very extensive attention in recent years.

The Notion of a Balanced-Budget Amendment

The issue of a balanced-budget amendment has been debated, at one level or another, for a number of years. This debate has, in part, contributed to the formulation of a number of proposals for a balanced-budget amendment. Most of these proposals are at least somewhat similar. Nevertheless, each proposal naturally tends to have one or more characteristics that to some degree differentiate it from the other proposals.

In order the provide the reader with the flavor of such proposals, two are presented here. These proposals, labeled below simply as "Proposal A" and "Proposal B," are theoretically under consideration in Congress. Naturally, the ultimate form of a balanced-budget amendment to the Constitution is unknown; indeed, such an amendment may never even materialize.

The version of the balanced-budget amendment presented below as "Proposal A" was drafted some years ago. Proposal A contains the following provisions:[1]

Section 1. Total government outlays in any fiscal year shall not exceed the spending limit. The spending limit is equal to the average of total budget receipts in the three most recent fiscal years.

Section 2. Total government outlays include all budget and off-budget expenditures plus the present value of commitments for future outlays.

Section 3. The rate of growth of total receipts in any fiscal year shall not exceed the average rate of growth of an appropriate index in the most recently completed calendar year. The index shall be chosen by Congress and may be changed by 2/3 vote of each house.

Section 4. In the event that an emergency is declared by the President, the Congress may by 2/3 vote of each house authorize outlays for that fiscal year in excess of the spending limit.

Section 5. Congress shall enact all necessary legislation to implement the amendment.

The version of the balanced-budget amendment presented below as "Proposal B" was introduced in the United States Senate on January 3, 1985. After being read, it was referred to the Senate's Committee on the Judiciary. According to Proposal B:

Section 1. Prior to each fiscal year, the Congress shall adopt a statement of receipts and outlays for that year in which total outlays are not greater than total receipts. The Congress may amend such statement provided revised outlays are not greater than revised receipts. Whenever three-fifths of the whole number of both Houses shall deem it necessary, Congress in such statement may provide for a specific excess of outlays over receipts by a vote directed solely to that subject. The Congress and the President shall ensure, pursuant to legislation or through exercise of their powers under the first and second articles, that actual outlays do not exceed the outlays set forth in such statement.

Section 2. Total receipts for any fiscal year set forth in the statement adopted pursuant to this article shall not increase by a rate greater than the rate of increase in national income in the year or years ending not less than six months nor more than twelve months before such fiscal year, unless a majority of the whole number of both Houses of Congress shall have passed a bill directed solely to approving specific additional receipts and such bill has become law.

Section 3. Prior to each fiscal year, the President shall transmit to Congress a proposed statement of receipts and outlays for that year consistent with the provisions of this article.

Section 4. The Congress may waive the provisions of this article for any fiscal year in which a declaration of war is in effect.

Section 5. Total receipts shall include all receipts of the United States except those derived from borrowing and total outlays shall include all outlays of the United States except those for repayment of debt principal.

Section 6. The Congress shall enforce and implement this article by appropriate legislation.

Section 7. This article shall take effect in the second fiscal year beginning after its ratification.

In principle, a balanced-budget amendment is a rule that (theoretically) attempts to limit the federal government's ability to run deficits. However, exceptions appear to be possible. Witness, for example, the provisions in Section 4 of Proposal A and in Sections 1 and 4 of Proposal B. Such caveats are fairly commonplace in balanced-budget proposals.

As appealing as balanced-budget amendments may be to many policy-makers, major questions remain regarding such amendments. To begin with, whether such an amendment will in fact ever be passed is not known. Despite an allegedly widespread concern over the deficit, congressional passage of one version or another of the balanced-budget amendment does not seem imminent. Indeed, even if the requisite portions of both houses of Congress should in fact pass some version of the amendment on to the states for ratification, it is unknown whether the requisite three-fourths of the states will in fact ratify it within the necessary seven-year period. Witness, for instance, the fate of the Equal Rights Amendment.

On another level, the possible effects of a balanced-budget amendment on the undertaking and effectiveness of traditional forms of discretionary fiscal policy may be cause for concern. Of course, until one knows the actual form of the amendment that is passed (*if* such an amendment is passed), one cannot address this issue rigorously. Nevertheless, it seems very likely that at least some significant limitations on the form and application of discretionary fiscal policies would be experienced under the type of amendment in question. This issue will be addressed in somewhat further detail at the end of this chapter.

Perhaps the most basic issue surrounding a balanced-budget amendment is whether it can in fact even work: Can such an amendment actually put an effective end to the pattern of federal budget deficits? Alternatively stated: Can a rule work effectively to control the growth over time of government spending, taxes, and deficits? That is: Is it possible to enact a rule that, if applied appropriately, can realistically be expected to reduce the growth (size) of government spending and hence, taxes and deficits? We technically do not know whether such rules do work. Nor do we seem to know whether these are rules that can work; that is, whether such rules can be effective. We simply cannot answer such questions with certainty. However, it is possible that at least some inferences can be made on the basis of experience at the nonfederal level with "tax-expenditure limitations." That is to say, the United States has had some experience (albeit limited) at the nonfederal level with statutory and constitutional measures; that is, with rules that have attempted to control government spending and taxes at the nonfederal level. Perhaps an examination of such rules will provide insights into the prospects of pursuing similar goals at the federal level via the route of a constitutional amendment, as well as insights into what some of the most fruitful forms of such an amendment would be.

Most of the remainder of this chapter uses simple simulation techniques to gain insight into the potential effectiveness of using a constitutional amendment to limit the growth of government outlays and taxation. None of the following analysis can yield truly definitive conclusions for the federal budget deficit problem. This inability to generate definitive conclusions is in part due to the nature of the simulation technique (which technique is explained below) and in part to the fact that we do not know the form of the final version of the federal balanced-budget amendment (if such an amendment is in fact even enacted). Nevertheless, the analysis that follows may provide at least tentative conclusions as to the potential usefulness of and potentially most useful form(s) of a balanced-budget amendment (rule). Hopefully, this chapter will be of some interest to those concerned not only with controlling government spending, taxes, and deficits at the federal level, but also to those concerned with controlling government spending and taxes (and perhaps deficits as well) at the nonfederal level.

Tax-Expenditure Limitations—An Initial Analysis

In 1976, New Jersey became the first state to impose a ceiling on the growth in state expenditures. The statute by which this was accomplished limited the growth in state expenditures to the growth in the state's per capita personal income.

After the approval of California's Proposition 13 in June of 1978, tax limitation efforts spread quickly to other states. At the present time, some seventeen states have tax-expenditure limitations (hereafter referred to simply as "TELs") in effect.[2] Moreover, this total of seventeen omits New Jersey, whose TEL expired in June of 1983, and Utah, where a TEL was passed in 1979 but, because of the failure to enact necessary supporting legislation, never went into effect.[3]

It is important to note that in no case do TELs cover the entirety of a state's revenues or expenditures. Typically, TELs do not limit expenditures that are outside of the general fund. Indeed, in a number of instances, even certain categories of spending in the general fund are ignored. Revenue sources excluded from the scope of TELs include bond revenue and federal aid.

There currently is no consensus as to the effectiveness of TELs. For example, studies by Gold (1983) and Bails (1982) have found TELs to be largely ineffective. Similarly, Kenyon and Benker (1984, p. 438) argue that "examination of both survey results and actual expenditure data indicates that, for most states, tax or expenditure limits have not been a constraint on growth in taxing or spending." By contrast, Shannon and Caulkins (1983) have found TELs to work effectively. For instance, Shannon and Caulkins (1983, p. 23) argue that the taxpayer's revolution of the 1978–1980 time period not only imposed explicit forms of tax and spending limits, but also conveyed a very powerful message to:

> state and local policymakers, most of whom escaped highly restrictive fiscal limitations. The message was clear: If you want to avoid Proposition 13-type restrictions, make sure that the increase in public spending does not exceed the growth of the private economy.

Using a simple simulation technique, this section of the chapter examines the potential effectiveness of one form of TELs in restraining the growth of government spending and hence taxes. More specifically, this section of the chapter examines the potential effectiveness of one form of TEL in slowing or reversing the growth trend in state and local government. The focus in this section of the chapter is upon California's well-known Proposition 4 and what the expenditure and tax effects would likely have been if Proposition 4 (or its equivalent) had been enacted in all of the fifty states plus the District of Columbia. The next section of this chapter examines an alternative simulation, a simulation based upon growth of per capita personal income.

Analysis

This section of the chapter examines what the government expenditure and tax burden impacts of Proposition 4 would likely have been if it (or its equivalent) had been enacted in all of the states and the District of Columbia. Since one cannot see into the future with any great degree of certainty on this issue, this section of the chapter attempts to gain insights by looking at the experiences of the recent past. Specifically, this section first examines what happened to *actual* state plus local government expenditures per capita over the period FY 1970 to FY 1976. Next examined is what presumably would have happened to state plus local government expenditures per capita if Proposition 4 (or its equivalent) had been in effect over the very same period. By contrasting these two sets of expenditure figures, one may gain insights into the potential impact of Proposition 4 (or its equivalent) on expenditure levels per capita (and thus on tax burdens per capita).

Column 1 of table 4–1 provides, according to state (and the District of Columbia), the per capita expenditures of state plus local government during FY 1970 (July 1, 1970 to June 30, 1971). Column 2 of table 4–1 provides, for the same area, the per capita expenditures of state plus local governments during FY 1976 (July 1, 1976 to June 30, 1977). As the table clearly indicates, this time period—a period of relatively high inflation rates in the United States—was in addition a period of rapidly rising per capita state plus local government spending.

Now consider the potential impact on state and local government spending for the same time period if Proposition 4 (or its equivalent) had been in effect in all of the fifty states plus the District of Columbia. Begin by referring to the following provision in Proposition 4:

> The total annual appropriations subject to limitation of the state and of each local government shall not exceed the appropriations limit of such entity of government for the prior year adjusted for changes in the cost of living and population except as otherwise provided in this Article.

Hence, this measure would have limited the per capita growth in state plus local government spending in each area to the percentage increase in the cost of living (aside from population considerations).

Several observations are now in order. First, the per capita state plus local government expenditures examined in this study consist strictly of direct general expenditures of state and local governments. Included in such outlays are direct expenditures by state and local governments per se on education, highways, public welfare, health and hospitals, policy protection, fire protection, natural resources, local parks and recreation, financial administration, sanitation, and interest on general debt. Second, it is assumed that the TEL under consideration, that is, Proposition 4, covers all direct general expenditures of state and local governments. Third, the cost-of-living measure that is generally accepted for the purpose of imposing an expenditure growth rate ceiling is the "consumer price index" (CPI). This in fact is the precise living-cost measure built into Proposition 4; hence, it is the one used in the following computations.[4] Fourth, the cited provision sets

Table 4–1
Actual and Theoretical Per Capita Expenditure Levels, by State, FY 1970 to FY 1976
(in current dollars)

State	Per Capita Expenditure 7/1/70–6/30/71 (1)	Per Capita Expenditure 7/1/76–6/30/77 (2)	Theoretical Per Capita Expenditure 7/1/76–6/30/77 (3)	Difference (2) − (3) (4)
Alabama	564	1,002	827	175
Alaska	1,828	3,275	2,680	595
Arizona	704	1,243	1,032	211
Arkansas	508	876	745	131
California	916	1,486	1,343	143
Colorado	728	1,346	1,067	279
Connecticut	790	1,152	1,158	−6
Delaware	921	1,458	1,350	108
District of Columbia	1,234	2,064	1,809	255
Florida	613	1,099	899	200
Georgia	616	1,003	903	100
Hawaii	1,126	1,915	1,651	264
Idaho	639	1,141	937	204
Illinois	711	1,266	1,042	224
Indiana	581	953	852	101
Iowa	690	1,235	1,012	223
Kansas	646	1,103	048	246
Kentucky	577	1,006	846	160
Louisiana	678	1,207	994	213
Maine	646	1,120	947	173
Maryland	780	1,453	1,144	309
Massachusetts	783	1,378	1,148	230
Michigan	757	1,390	1,110	280
Minnesota	806	1,460	1,182	278
Mississippi	595	1,018	872	146
Missouri	606	942	888	54
Montana	754	1,409	1,105	304
Nebraska	649	1,153	952	201
Nevada	956	1,470	1,402	68
New Hampshire	615	1,116	902	214
New Jersey	711	1,327	1,042	285
New Mexico	717	1,177	1,051	126
New York	1,075	1,795	1,576	219
North Carolina	527	982	773	209
North Dakota	726	1,308	1,064	244
Ohio	584	1,109	856	253
Oklahoma	623	1,045	913	132
Oregon	756	1,414	1,108	306
Pennsylvania	681	1,166	998	168
Rhode Island	687	1,283	1,007	276
South Carolina	501	979	735	244
South Dakota	724	1,180	1,061	119
Tennessee	570	992	836	156
Texas	564	1,003	827	176
Utah	677	1,201	993	208
Vermont	840	1,280	1,232	48

Table 4–1 continued

State	Per Capita Expenditure 7/1/70–6/30/71 (1)	Per Capita Expenditure 7/1/76–6/30/77 (2)	Theoretical Per Capita Expenditure 7/1/76–6/30/77 (3)	Difference (2) − (3) (4)
Virginia	593	1,105	869	236
Washington	880	1,357	1,290	67
West Virginia	634	1,083	930	153
Wisconsin	764	1,322	1,120	202
Wyoming	940	1,572	1,378	194

Source: U.S. Bureau of the Census, *Statistical Abstract of the United States, 1978,* Washington, D.C., 1978, Table 673.

a ceiling on most forms of state and local government spending. Hence, it is conceivable that state and local governments could increase their spending levels (per capita) by an amount less than the growth in the CPI.[5] Nevertheless, since there is no guarantee that they would in fact not go to the limit, in the computations provided below it is arbitrarily assumed that, in each area, per capita expenditures will grow by the maximum permitted under Proposition 4 (or its equivalent). Finally, it is assumed here that none of the state or local governments will invoke their so-called emergency clauses to authorize spending beyond the established ceiling.[6]

Let Mi be the maximum amount by which per capita nominal state plus local government expenditures in area i could have increased from FY 1970 to FY 1976, according to Proposition 4 (or its equivalent). To calculate Mi, perform the following computation for each of the fifty states, as well as the District of Columbia:

$$Mi = Ei_{(1970)} \cdot \Delta P_{(1970-76)}, i = 1, \ldots, 51, \qquad (4.1)$$

where $Ei_{(1970)}$ is per capita state plus local government expenditures in area i, FY 1970; and $\Delta P_{(1970-76)}$ is percentage change in the CPI, FY 1970–FY 1976.

The value of $\Delta P_{(1970-76)}$ is given by the following:

$$\Delta P_{(1970-76)} = \frac{171.1 - 116.7}{116.7} = .46615, \qquad (4.2)$$

where the base year is 1967 (1967 = 100.0).

In column 3 of table 4–1, the value of Mi for each state and the District of Columbia has been added to the level of Ei for each of these fifty-one areas. Therefore, the figures in column 3 represent the theoretical maximum total level per capita to which Proposition 4 would have allowed, in each individual case, state plus local government expenditures to rise over the period in question.

Column 4 shows the differences between columns 2 and 3; that is, the value of the spending level in column 2 minus that in column 3 in each case. A positive (negative) value for any given area in column 4 implies that, under Proposition 4, per capita state plus local government spending would have been lower (higher) than actually was the case.

Column 4 of table 4–1 indicates that, except for one case (Connecticut), the existence of Proposition 4 would theoretically have yielded lower per capita state plus local government spending for FY 1976. In other words, in fifty out of the fifty-one cases, Proposition 4 (or its equivalent) theoretically would have lowered per capita state plus local government expenditures. Such a conclusion may be misleading, however. That is, the simple observation of a consistent pattern of differences does not necessarily imply that there is a statistically significant difference between the two sets of spending figures as a whole. Consequently, the next step in the analysis is to test formally whether there is in fact a statistically significant difference between the average hypothetical FY 1976 per capita government spending level under Proposition 4 and the average actual FY 1976 per capita government spending level.

Begin by stating the following test:

$$t = \frac{D}{S_D/\sqrt{N}}, \tag{4.3}$$

where D is the difference in the population means; S_D is the difference in the population standard deviations; and N is population size. Note that the populations for columns 2 and 3 of table 4–1 are identical.

The necessary data to make the computations in equation 4.3 is as follows. Specifically, the mean actual per capita expenditure level is $1,284.49, whereas the mean theoretical per capita expenditure level is $1,086.37. The standard deviation for actual per capita expenditures is $373.09, whereas the standard deviation for theoretical per capita expenditures is $320.75.

On the basis of this data, it follows that

$$D = 1,284.49 - 1,086.37 = 198.12 \tag{4.4}$$

and

$$S_D = 373.09 - 320.75 = 52.34 \tag{4.5}$$

Substituting from equations 4.4 and 4.5 into equation 4.3 yields

$$t = \frac{198.12}{52.34\sqrt{51}} = \frac{198.12}{52.34/7.14} = 27.025 \tag{4.6}$$

The null hypothesis is given by

$$H_o : \Delta = 0 \tag{4.7}$$

where Δ represents the mean difference between the actual and estimated (that is, theoretical) expenditure levels in FY 1976.

Clearly, the t-value in equation 4.6 causes the rejection of the null hypothesis at far beyond the 99 percent confidence level. Thus, under the assumption that state and local government units would have spent up to their legal limits under Proposition 4, it has been found here that, for the period studied (FY 1970 to FY 1976), the existence of a rule (in this case, Proposition 4) could have resulted in a statistically significant reduction in per capita nominal state plus local government spending. In turn, this finding is of very obvious importance to taxpayers, as indicated by the following provision in Proposition 4:

> Revenues received by an entity of government in excess of that amount which is appropriated by such entity in compliance with this Article during the fiscal year shall be returned by a revision of tax rates or fee schedules.

Hence, the principal tax implication of the results in this section of the chapter is that, for the period considered, Proposition 4 could presumably have lead to a statistically significant reduction in tax levels per capita (where taxes are also measured in nominal terms).[7]

In conclusion, from this analysis of the period from FY 1970 to FY 1976, one can infer that rules (TELs) may indeed offer promise for reducing the growth rates (per capita) of both state plus local government nominal spending and state plus local government nominal tax collections. This conclusion may lead to a degree of guarded optimism for the use of an inflation-based form of balanced-budget amendment to control the federal budget. In other words, there may be reason to believe that we may be able to control the government budget by tying the hands of government officials with a constitutional amendment using a restriction based on inflation. Such an amendment (TEL) apparently could potentially have worked at the nonfederal level.

Tax-Expenditure Limitations—An Alternative Analysis

The conclusions in the preceding section of this chapter are based upon a TEL that restricts the growth in per capita state plus local government spending to the inflation rate of the consumer price index. Such a basis for limiting the growth of government outlays (and hence taxes) is predicated upon California's well-known Proposition 4. However, it may well be appropriate to address the possibility of restricting the growth rate of government spending to the growth rate of per capita personal income. Indeed, in 1976, New Jersey enacted a statute that limited the growth in state expenditures to the growth in the state's level of per capita personal income; since 1976, a number of other states have enacted TELs having a similar basis for the limitation of government expenditure growth.

Analysis

In this section of the chapter, the impact of restricting the growth rate in per capita state plus local government spending to the growth rate in per capita personal income is examined. For all reasonable intents and purposes, the analysis in this section methodologically parallels that in the preceding section except that: (1) this analysis uses the growth rate of per capita personal income rather than the inflation rate of the consumer price index as the basis for the government spending limitation; and (2) it uses the per capita personal income growth rate for each individual area rather than the average per capita personal income growth rate for the nation as a whole.

Let Vi be the maximum amount by which per capita state plus local government spending in area i could have increased from FY 1970 to FY 1976 if Vi were limited by the growth rate in area i's per capita personal income over the same time period. To calculate $Vi, i = 1, \ldots, 51$, perform the following calculation for each of the fifty states, as well as the District of Columbia:

$$Vi = Ei_{(1970)} \cdot \Delta YPCi_{(1970-76)}, \tag{4.8}$$

where Ei is per capita state plus local government expenditures in area i, FY 1970; and $\Delta YPCi$ is percentage rate of change (growth) in area i's per capita personal income, from 1970–76. Observe that a separate calculation must be made for each of the fifty-one areas considered; furthermore, each such calculation involves each individual area's own initial spending level (Ei) and own unique growth rate of per capita personal income ($\Delta YPCi$).

Column 1 of table 4–2 provides the per capita personal income in each state in 1970, whereas column 2 of table 4–2 provides the per capita personal income in each state for the year 1976. Finally, column 3 of table 4–2 provides, for each state, the decimal corresponding to $\Delta YPCi$. Thus, column 3 of the table provides, for each individual area, the growth rate of that area's per capita personal income over the 1970 to 1976 period.

Column 1 of table 4–3 provides the actual level of FY 1976 per capita state plus local government spending for each of the fifty-one areas studied.

Table 4–2
Per Capita Personal Income, by State, 1970 and 1976
(in current dollars)

State	Per Capita Personal Income, by State, 1970 ($) (1)	Per Capita Personal Income, by State, 1976 ($) (2)	Growth Rate (3)
Alabama	2,948	5,105	.732
Alaska	4,644	10,178	1.192
Arizona	3,665	5,817	.587
Arkansas	2,878	5,073	.763
California	4,493	7,164	.594
Colorado	3,855	6,503	.687
Connecticut	4,917	7,373	.499
Delaware	4,524	7,290	.611
District of Columbia	5,079	8,648	.703
Florida	3,738	6,108	.636
Georgia	3,354	5,571	.661
Hawaii	4,623	6,969	.507
Idaho	3,290	5,726	.740
Illinois	4,507	7,432	.649
Indiana	3,772	6,257	.659
Iowa	3,751	6,439	.717
Kansas	3,853	6,495	.660
Kentucky	3,112	5,423	.743
Louisiana	3,090	5,386	.743
Maine	3,302	5,385	.631
Maryland	4,309	7,036	.633
Massachusetts	4,340	6,585	.517
Michigan	4,180	6,994	.673
Minnesota	3,859	6,153	.594
Mississippi	2,626	4,575	.742
Missouri	3,781	6,005	.588
Montana	3,500	5,600	.600
Nebraska	3,789	6,240	.647
Nevada	4,563	7,337	.608
New Hampshire	3,737	5,973	.598
New Jersey	4,701	7,269	.546
New Mexico	3,077	5,213	.694
New York	4,712	7,100	.507
North Carolina	3,252	5,409	.663
North Dakota	3,086	5,400	.750
Ohio	4,020	6,432	.600
Oklahoma	3,387	5,657	.670
Oregon	3,719	6,331	.702
Pennsylvania	3,971	6,466	.628
Rhode Island	3,959	6,498	.641
South Carolina	2,990	5,126	.714
South Dakota	3,123	4,796	.536
Tennessee	3,119	5,432	.742
Texas	3,606	6,243	.731
Utah	3,227	5,482	.699
Vermont	3,468	5,480	.580
Virginia	3,712	6,276	.691
Washington	4,053	6,772	.671

Table 4–2 continued

State	Per Capita Personal Income, by State, 1970 ($) (1)	Per Capita Personal Income, by State, 1976 ($) (2)	Growth Rate (3)
West Virginia	3,061	5,394	.762
Wisconsin	3,812	6,293	.651
Wyoming	3,815	6,723	.762

Source: U.S. Bureau of the Census, Statistical Abstract of the United States, 1984, Washington, D.C., 1984, Table 772.

Based upon the data in column 3 of table 4–2, column 2 of table 4–3 provides the theoretical level of FY 1976 per capita state plus local government expenditures for each of the fifty-one areas studied. The numbers shown in column 2 of table 4–3, Ui, were computed as follows:

$$Ui = Ei + Vi = Ei(1 + \Delta YPCi), i = 1, \ldots , 51, \qquad (4.9)$$

where Ui is the *theoretical* total level of FY 1976 per capita state plus local government spending in area i.

Meanwhile, column 3 of table 4–3 shows the difference, for each of the fifty-one areas studied, between the actual level and the theoretical level shown in columns 1 and 2, respectively. A *positive* value in column 3 indicates that the TEL under examination theoretically would have generated a reduced per capita state plus local government spending level. On the other hand, a *negative* value in column 3 indicates that the TEL in question would theoretically have elevated that spending level. On the basis of the computations shown in table 4–3, there are a total of thirty-four positive values and a total of sixteen negative values, with one case (Kentucky) having a zero value.[8]

Hence, it would appear that, in most cases (roughly 67 percent), the TEL would seemingly have been effective in reducing government outlays. On the other hand, there were a number of cases (nearly 32 percent) in which the TEL would seemingly have been ineffective. Note also the special case of Alaska, where the TEL in question would have permitted an additional $732 per capita in state plus local government spending in FY 1976. In the Alaska case, it just turns out that there was an enormous rise (in excess of 119 percent) in per capita personal income over the period in question. In the interest of not distorting the population average and standard deviation with the inclusion of this special case, Alaska shall be excluded from the calculations and the following will deal with an N equal in size to fifty.[9]

Table 4–3
Actual and Theoretical Expenditure Levels, by State, FY 1976
(in current dollars)

State	Actual Per Capita Expenditure 7/1/76–6/30/77 (1)	Theoretical Per Capita Expenditure 7/1/76–6/30/77 (2)	Difference (1) − (2) (3)
Alabama	1,002	920	82
Alaska	3,275	4,007	−732
Arizona	1,243	1,117	126
Arkansas	876	896	−20
California	1,486	1,466	20
Colorado	1,346	1,228	118
Connecticut	1,152	1,184	−32
Delaware	1,458	1,484	−26
District of Columbia	2,064	2,102	−38
Florida	1,099	1,003	96
Georgia	1,003	1,023	−20
Hawaii	1,915	1,697	218
Idaho	1,141	1,112	29
Illinois	1,266	1,172	94
Indiana	953	964	−11
Iowa	1,235	1,185	50
Kansas	1,103	1,072	31
Kentucky	1,006	1,006	0
Louisiana	1,207	1,182	25
Maine	1,120	1,054	66
Maryland	1,453	1,274	179
Massachusetts	1,378	1,188	190
Michigan	1,390	1,266	124
Minnesota	1,460	1,285	175
Mississippi	1,018	1,036	−18
Missouri	942	962	−20
Montana	1,409	1,206	203
Nebraska	1,153	1,069	84
Nevada	1,470	1,537	−67
New Hampshire	1,116	983	178
New Jersey	1,327	1,099	228
New Mexico	1,177	1,215	−38
New York	1,795	1,620	175
North Carolina	982	876	106
North Dakota	1,308	1,271	37
Ohio	1,109	934	175
Oklahoma	1,045	1,040	5
Oregon	1,414	1,287	127
Pennsylvania	1,166	1,109	57
Rhode Island	1,283	1,122	161
South Carolina	979	859	120
South Dakota	1,180	1,112	68
Tennessee	992	993	−1
Texas	1,003	976	27
Utah	1,201	1,150	51
Vermont	1,280	1,327	−47
Virginia	1,105	1,003	102

Table 4–3 continued

State	Actual Per Capita Expenditure 7/1/76–6/30/77 (1)	Theoretical Per Capita Expenditure 7/1/76–6/30/77 (2)	Difference (1) – (2) (3)
Washington	1,357	1,470	−113
West Virginia	1,083	1,117	−34
Wisconsin	1,322	1,261	61
Wyoming	1,572	1,656	−84

Source: U.S. Bureau of the Census, *Statistical Abstract of the United States, 1978,* Washington, D.C., 1978, Table 673.

In order to formally test the impact of the TEL in question, once again refer to the following formulation:

$$t = \frac{D}{S_D/\sqrt{N}} \tag{4.10}$$

With the state of Alaska excluded from the analysis, the means for columns (1) and (2) of table 4–3 are $1,244.68 and $1,183.41, respectively, whereas the standard deviations for columns (1) and (2) of table 4–3 are $244.05 and $238.50, respectively. Substituting these values into 4.10 yields:

$$D = 1244.68 - 1183.41 = 61.27 \tag{4.11}$$

$$S_D = 244.05 - 238.50 = 5.55 \tag{4.12}$$

Substituting from equations 4.11 and 4.12 into equation 4.10 yields:

$$t = \frac{61.27}{5.55/\sqrt{50}} = \frac{61.27}{5.55/7.08} = 78.151 \tag{4.13}$$

The null hypothesis is given by

$$H_o : \Delta = 0, \tag{4.14}$$

where Δ is the mean difference between the actual and theoretical expenditure levels in FY 1976.

Clearly, the *t*-value in equation 4.13 causes the rejection of the null hypothesis in 4.14 at far beyond the 99 percent confidence level. The implications of this form of TEL (rule) for controlling the growth of per capita government spending (and taxes) are similar to those already presented at the end of the preceding section of this chapter.

At least three closing remarks are now in order. First, both forms of TEL (rule) explicitly considered thus far in this chapter could theoretically have effectively limited the growth of government spending, at least to some degree. Second, although the two simulations examined here are very similar, they are certainly not identical. Perhaps the most important difference between the two simulations is that one simulation is tied to a single number for all areas, namely, the inflation rate of the consumer price index nationally, whereas the other simulation is tied to a different number for each area, namely, the growth rate of that particular area's per capita personal income. Third, although not presented here for reasons of space (the analysis would necessarily be rather lengthy) and because the results are compelling but not entirely conclusive (due to certain data limitations), a number of regressions have been estimated to test the effectiveness of TELs. Most of these regressions, with a dummy variable indicating the presence or absence of a TEL, indicate that TELs had a reasonably significant negative impact upon the growth rate of per capita real state plus local government spending for the period from 1977 to 1981.

The Federal Case: Applying the TELs

It may now be appropriate to examine what the impact upon the federal budget would theoretically have been if rules such as those examined in the two preceding sections of this chapter were enacted. In other words, for the period FY 1970 to FY 1976, now examine what would presumably have been the effect of: (1) a TEL limiting the growth rate of per capita federal government spending to the inflation rate of the consumer price index and (2) a TEL limiting the growth rate of per capita federal government spending to the growth rate of a per capita personal income. A third rule will also be considered in this section of the chapter.

The first problem to be addressed is that of determining the scope of federal government spending to be placed under the limitation. Clearly, this will ultimately depend upon the final form of the balanced-budget amendment that is enacted (if such an amendment is enacted). On the basis of balanced-budget Proposal A, total federal government outlays would include all budget and off-budget expenditures plus the present value of commitments for future outlays. On the basis of Proposal B, total federal government outlays would include all outlays of the United States except those for repayment of the national debt principal.

For simplicity, the federal government outlays to be subject to limitation are defined as consisting of all budget outlays plus all off-budget outlays. For FY 1970 and FY 1976, table 4–4 provides the actual levels of total federal government outlays so defined.[10] Table 4–4 also provides, for FY

Table 4–4
Federal Outlays, Total and Per Capita

	FY 1970	FY 1976
Actual Federal Outlays[a]	195.7	371.8
Actual Per Capita Federal Outlays[b]	960.02	1,712.61
Theoretical Per Capita Federal Outlays, Inflation Method[b]	—	1,407.53
Theoretical Total Federal Outlays, Inflation Method[a]	—	305.6
Theoretical Net Reduction in Total Federal Outlays, Inflation Method[a]	—	66.2

Source: U.S. Bureau of the Census, *Statistical Abstract of the United States, 1984,* Washington, D.C., 1984, Table 498.
[a]Billions of current dollars.
[b]Current dollars.

1970 and FY 1976, the actual levels of per capita federal outlays. Using the inflation factor provided in equation 4.2 of 0.46615, table 4–4 provides the theoretical per capita level of federal government outlays resulting from the "inflation method," that is, the restricting of the growth rate of per capita government spending to the inflation rate of the consumer price index. As table 4–4 shows, application of the TEL method (rule) of limiting the growth rate of per capita federal outlays to the inflation rate of the consumer price index seems to reduce total federal spending in FY 1976 by 66.2 billion current collars. The saving is less if population is accounted for.

In table 4–5, the "per capita income method" form of TEL is applied; that is, the restricting of the growth rate of per capita government outlays to the percentage growth rate of per capita personal income. Per capita personal income in the United States as a whole grew by 61.1 percent over the period from 1970 to 1976. Table 4–5 shows that if the growth rate of

Table 4–5
The Pattern of Federal Outlays, Total and Per Capita

	FY 1970	FY 1976
Actual Federal Outlays[a]	195.7	371.8
Actual Per Capita Federal Outlays[b]	960.02	1,712.61
Theoretical Per Capita Federal Outlays, Per Capita Income Method[b]	—	1,546.59
Theoretical Total Federal Outlays, Per Capita Income Method[a]	—	335.8
Theoretical Net Reduction in Total Federal Outlays, Per Capita Income Method[a]	—	36.0

Source: U.S. Bureau of the Census, *Statistical Abstract of the United States, 1984,* Washington, D.C., 1984, Table 498.
[a]Billions of current dollars.
[b]Current dollars.

per capita total federal government outlays is limited to the growth rate of per capita personal income, then the theoretical per capita level of total federal outlays in FY 1976 is reduced from $1,712.61 to $1,546.59. This reduction in turn translates into a theoretical net reduction in the total federal outlays in FY 1976 of 36.0 billion current dollars, given the population.

Tables 4–4 and 4–5 have considered the theoretical impact of two possible forms of TEL (rule) on total federal outlays for the period FY 1970 to FY 1976. In each case, it appeared that the strict application of the TEL in question achieved a noticeable reduction in total federal outlays.[11] This conclusion parallels that obtained earlier in this chapter for these same two forms of TEL. The reader may wish to verify the fact that the strict application of either of the two forms of TEL in question through the current time period would have generated the same basic conclusion.[12] Moreover, this basic conclusion also is sustained for most alternative definitions of the federal outlays to be limited by the TELs in question.

Of course, there are alternatives to the so-called inflation method and to the so-called per capita income method. One such alternative would be to limit the rate of growth in total federal government outlays to the rate of growth of national income. In effect, this rule is consistent with Section 2 of balanced-budget Proposal B. Table 4–6 provides actual and theoretical levels of total federal government outlays for FY 1970, FY 1976, and, to be more current, FY 1982. As shown in the table, this rule of limiting the growth rate in total federal spending to the growth rate of national income would apparently have yielded a theoretical reduction in total federal outlays of 38.5 billion current dollars in FY 1976 and a theoretical reduction of 76.8 billion current dollars in FY 1982.

Concluding Remarks

This chapter has attempted to provide insights to help determine whether rules intended to control the growth of government spending and, hence,

Table 4–6
The Pattern of Total Federal Outlays
(Billions of current dollars)

	FY 1970	FY 1976	FY 1982
Actual Total Federal Outlays	195.7	371.8	745.7
Theoretical Total Federal Outlays	—	333.3	668.9
Theoretical Reduction in Total Federal Outlays	—	38.5	76.8
National Income	798.4	1,359.8	2,446.8

Source: U.S. Bureau of the Census, *Statistical Abstract of the United States, 1984,* Washington, D.C., 1984, Table 498.

taxes can theoretically work. Ultimately, of course, the concern is over whether, through the control of government spending and taxes, a balanced-budget amendment to the U.S. Constitution could theoretically achieve its alleged objective.

Perhaps the most basic question to address is whether rules meant to control government spending can work. On the basis of the two simulations involving per capita state and local government spending and on the basis of the three essentially parallel but briefer simulations involving total federal government spending or per capita total federal government spending, it seems that such rules potentially can be successful. That is, such rules, if applied strictly, theoretically can reduce measurably the growth of government spending. In fact, this chapter's analysis has identified at least three specific rules that, if strictly applied, could theoretically do the job effectively. Moreover, although not examined here, other rules can be shown to be potentially effective as well.

The next basic question is, given that at least certain specific rules theoretically can succeed at reducing the growth of government spending, under what circumstances will they fail to do so? To begin with, it is clear that the choice of rule is critical. That is, if government spending growth is somehow limited by the growth of a factor that grows much more rapidly than, say, per capita personal income, then government spending growth could either exceed existing patterns or simply fail to be significantly reduced.

A probably more significant threat to the potential effectiveness of rules is the so-called emergency clause. Such a clause is explicitly included in Section 4 of Proposal A. Moreover, "exceptions" or "escape clauses" are found in Sections 1 and 4 of Proposal B. The problem at hand is very real. Such emergency clauses, exceptions clauses, and escape clauses are a common feature of TELs and of proposed balanced-budget amendments.

It is entirely possible (if not probable) that even a recession, particularly if severe, could constitute an emergency or exception. Indeed, the word "emergency" can be so interpreted as to apply to a wide range of possible (if not common) circumstances or conditions. Accordingly, such clauses potentially could convert a balanced-budget amendment into useless rhetoric. Indeed, the need for concern on this point is echoed by Bails (1982, p. 138), who, after analyzing a TEL in the state of Arizona, alleges that "escape clauses give political decision makers a device by which the limitation can be exceeded with relative ease."

Assuming that a rule is established and well chosen, that it is strictly applied, and that emergency clauses are not abused, the federal budget would generally be balanced, even during times of recession. To at least some significant degree, then, fiscal policy loses flexibility to cope with the business cycle. Moreover, the debilitating effects of the rule may not be restricted to discretionary fiscal policy. Indeed, the economy possesses automatic stabilizers, such as the income tax and unemployment compensation, which change automatically in response to the economy. As a result, they tend to moderate the upturns and downturns that the economy experiences over the course of the business cycle. Consider now Proposal B. Such a rule, by requiring a balanced budget, essentially ensures that even the automatic stabilizers will be or may be neutralized—for if the budget is going into deficit because of automatic stabilizers, it requires (according to Section 1) a three-fifths majority to permit that deficit. Otherwise taxes have to be increased or other forms of government spending must be cut. This trait of Proposal B and other such proposals is widely believed to be a major shortcoming.

In sum, then, state and local data have provided insights as to whether a set of rules allegedly directed at slowing the growth of government spending and taxes can, at least in theory, succeed. There in fact have been two simulations using state and local data; each simulation corresponded to an actually enacted state constitutional amendment or statute. In each case it was determined that such a rule theoretically could have successfully reduced state plus local government spending (and hence state plus local government taxes) in most cases. These findings thus created an optimism that, in theory, rules to limit government spending (and taxes) can potentially work. Applying these same two rules, plus a third rather similar rule, to the federal budget generated the same basic conclusion, namely, such rules can potentially work to limit the growth of federal government spending and taxes. Accordingly, one may infer that such rules may be useful to the pursuit of a balanced federal budget.

While those interested in state and local government finances as well as those interested in a balanced-budget amendment may view these findings as relevant, they must not lose sight of the potentially adverse impact of emergency clauses, escape clauses, and exception clauses in any rule that might be established. Finally, one must also be cognizant of the potentially very negative implications, at the federal level, of any rule for contracyclical fiscal policy effectiveness.

Notes

1. Related to this version of the balanced-budget amendment, see Aranson (1981, pp. 671–72).

2. These TELs are different from the so-called Rainy Day Funds, or RDFs, which are merely contingency funds. RDFs are found in some nineteen states.

3. As Gold (1984, p. 422) notes, "Eight TELs are constitutional, and the rest are set forth in statutes."

4. The appropriateness of using the CPI rather than an alternative price index is not debated here.

5. Related to this, see the remarks by Gold (1984, p. 429).

6. For simplicity, spending growth is assumed to be restricted solely by the inflation rate of the CPI; the issue of population size (and changes therein) is not dealt with here.

7. It is implicit that there is not a significant decline or increase in the magnitude of federal aid to state and local governments. Also, in choosing to study a period prior to FY 1977, this chapter does not study a period in which actual state plus local outlays may have been affected by the tax revolt.

8. A value of zero indicates no difference, that is, no change as a result of the TEL in question.

9. In the figures shown in table 4–1, the inflation rate was uniform for all of the states. However, if the actual inflation rate in Alaska paralleled Alaska's growth rate of per capita personal income, a set of computations based on that premise would likely have required also extricating Alaska from the calculations in equations 4.4, 4.5, and 4.6.

10. These figures do include off-budget outlays.

11. Of course, in the case of state and local governments, the existence of means *and* standard deviations allows formal testing for statistically significant differences in those means. No such comparison is technically possible in the federal case, however.

12. Implicitly, "emergency clauses," "escape clauses," and "exceptions clauses" have been ignored. These items are discussed later in this chapter.

References

Aranson, P.H. 1981. *American Government: Strategy and Choice*. Cambridge, Mass.: Winthrop Publishers.

Bails, D. 1982. "A Critique on the Effectiveness of Tax-Expenditure Limitations." *Public Choice* Vol. 38, No. 2: 129–138.

Gold, S.D. 1983. "State Tax and Spending Limitations: Paper Tigers or Slumbering Giants?" Legislative Finance Paper no. 33, National Conference of State Legislatures, Denver, Colorado.

——— 1984. "Contingency Measures and Fiscal Limitations: The Real World Significance of Some Recent State Budget Innovations." *National Tax Journal*, Vol. 37, No. 3, 421–32.

Kenyon, D.A. and Benker, K.M. 1984. "Fiscal Discipline: Lessons from the State Experience." National Tax Journal Vol. 37, No. 3, 433–46.

Ladd, H. 1978. "An Economic Evaluation of State Limitations on Local Taxing and Spending Powers." *National Tax Journal* Vol. 31, No. 1, 1–18.

Ladd, H. and Wilson, J.B. 1983. "Who Supports Tax Limitations: Evidence from Massachusetts Proposition 2 1/2." *Journal of Policy Analysis and Management* Vol. 20, No. 1, pp. 256–79.

Shannon, J. and Caulkins, S.E. 1983. "Federal and State-Local Spenders Go Their Separate Ways." *Intergovernmental Perspective* Vol. 8, Winter, 23–29.

Shapiro, P. and Morgan, W.E. 1978. "The General Revenue Effects of the California Tax Limitation Amendment." *National Tax Journal*, Vol. 31, No. 2, 199–228.

Stein, R.M., Hamm, K.E., and Freeman, P.K. 1983. "An Analysis of Support for Tax Limitation Referenda." *Public Choice*, Vol. 40, No. 2, pp. 187–94.

5
Coping with the Deficit and the Deficit Put into Perspective

C hapter 2 developed the basic analytical frame of reference for understanding the crowding out phenomenon. Several different possible forms of crowding out were identified and summarized. Indeed, there are even other possible forms of crowding out that could have been examined. In any event, on the basis of the theoretical literature, one can infer that crowding out is "complete," "zero," or "partial."

Chapter 3 deals empirically with the effects of federal budget deficits. The chapter shows that federal deficits do act to elevate the interest rate yield on three-month Treasury bills and on ten-year Treasury notes. These results are compatible with Barth, Iden, and Russek (1985), with an earlier study by Feldstein and Eckstein (1970), and with the following commentary by Cagan (1985, p. 205): "The market mechanism for accommodating sources and uses of funds to an increase in federal deficits is a rise in interest rates." In point of fact, the empirical results in chapter 3 indicate that just this sort of interest rate outcome is to be expected. Of course, as noted earlier, this finding is at odds with a good number of other studies, including studies by Evans (1985), Hoelscher (1983), Makin (1983), Mascaro and Meltzer (1983), and Motley (1983), just to name a few.

If in fact one can infer from the empirical analysis in chapter 3 that deficits do act to elevate interest rates, the next issue at hand becomes a quantitative one. And, as Cagan (1985) and Barth, Iden, and Russek (1984) observe, there are at least two very different views on this issue: The interest rate increase will be minor or the interest rate increase will be substantial. The attempt to definitively resolve this issue will not be made here. Nevertheless, the relevant findings by Cagan (1985) may be viewed here. Cagan finds the interest rate increase resulting from deficit financing to be neither minimal nor extremely high. Chapter 3 gave us the same result.

If one accepts this middle-of-the-road appraisal, then it would seem logical and reasonable to also accept a middle-of-the-road appraisal of crowding out. Namely, although crowding out does occur, it is definitely not complete; that is, only partial crowding out occurs. This assessment of partial crowding out is consistent with recent studies by Cebula (1985), Cagan (1985), Abrams and Schmitz (1978), Arestis (1979), and Zahn (1978).

Thus, despite the great public concern over federal budget deficits, the evidence implies that, although there are in fact adverse side effects from those deficits, these negative side effects have not been catastrophic. It is perhaps a bit ironic then that there is such a great public clamor for action to control the deficit. On the one hand, this clamor is weakly founded since there is no evidence of any disastrous side effects to date from the deficits. On the other hand, it should be observed that many economists (and others) are concerned that the financing and economic impacts of federal deficits appear to be somewhat unstable and that it is unclear as to how long the credit markets will be able to continue to absorb large volumes of Treasury borrowings in the future without greater adverse side effects. As Cagan (1985, p. 218) observes, although there has been evidence of only partial crowding out to date, this situation could change.

The great public clamor for deficit control has led to an intensified discussion of means by which to eliminate the "deficit problem." Chapter 4 in fact dealt with the possible usefulness of a balanced budget amendment. It argued that such a measure could potentially be useful, but such factors as emergency clauses raise significant doubts. There are, of course, alternative means by which to attempt to control the deficit. Indeed, the Gramm-Rudman-Hollings Act, passed by Congress in 1985, attests to the alleged willingness of our elected officials to address the deficit problem outside the explicit arena of a constitutional amendment. To a large extent, the remainder of this chapter addresses various alternatives (to the constitutional amendment approach) by which to potentially control or limit the deficit. The analysis that follows will be in general terms, with the objective being simply to highlight certain basic issues and problems.

Tax Policy

The current issue of tax policy seems to be broken into two possible forms: tax increases to raise revenues to lower the deficit; and tax reform.

In the absence of a detailed piece of actually enacted or at least approved legislation, it is extremely difficult (if not impossible) to definitively portray the long- or short-term effects of a policy of tax increases. Suffice it to say that if a tax increase is enacted it can act to reduce the growth of disposable income (directly or indirectly) and thus to reduce the growth of private sector spending. If this should happen, the possibility of either an economic slowdown or recession arises. And a slowdown or a recession could act to reduce the growth in actual tax collections by reducing the growth rate or size of the tax base. For example, even if a higher tax rate structure is put into effect, if it is applied to a diminished base or a more slowly growing base, lower tax collections than would originally have been collected might result. Or, alternatively, tax revenues simply may not grow by as much as was initially projected (although they may still, on balance, grow). In any event, given the accompanying growth in transfer payments that might be expected during an economic slowdown or recession, the deficit situation obviously may not improve appreciably.[1] Yet the private sector could pay a painful price for the policy experiment of raising taxes. Despite such perils, however, people like David Stockman (1986, p. 394) persist in demanding "a lot of new taxes to pay for the government the nation has decided it wants."

As for tax reform, several different proposals have appeared since 1981. For example, Senator William Bradley and Representative Richard Gephart introduced tax overhaul legislation in 1982. In April 1984, Representative Jack Kemp and Senator Robert Kasten introduced a different version of tax overhaul. The proposal, dubbed "Treasury I," was formally unveiled on November 27, 1984. Treasury I was the Treasury Department's response to President Reagan's January 1984 order to study tax reform. The Reagan administration formally announced its own proposal (called "Treasury II") on May 27, 1985. Most observers have argued that the federal tax system traditionally changes in increments and that tax policy changes commonly reflect the demands of major special interest groups (see, for example, Reese [1980] or Surrey [1957]) and/or various politicians whose ideology involves "unobtrusively encouraging market-based, non-zero-sum economic growth" (see King [1978, p. 25]). The proposals known as Treasury I and Treasury II, however, were quite different in that they proposed comprehensive change unpopular with many powerful associations of special interest groups and allegedly were targeted at achieving "equity" as opposed to providing capital incentives or other economic or social goals.

In 1985, President Reagan implored Congress to follow his lead to the achievement of a reformed federal income tax system. He requested passage of Treasury II, arguing among other things that it would be, essentially, "revenue neutral"; that is, it would presumably generate the same essential revenues as existing tax law over a five-year period. Note, in this time of alleged concern over deficits and raising more tax revenues, the irony of proposing a tax reform (as opposed to an increase) that is simply (and allegedly) only revenue neutral. Of course, a reformed tax system with its presumably lower tax rates might be an easier target for politicians to take aim at when (and if) they choose in the future to raise taxes.

In any event, on December 17, 1985, the House passed its version of a tax reform bill. The House version included a top individual income tax rate of 38 percent (Treasury II's top rate was 35 percent) and expected more taxes to be paid by the business sector of the economy than Treasury II did. In 1986, the Senate approached the tax overhaul issue. In April 1986, Senator Robert Packwood unveiled a tax reform plan with a top individual tax rate of 27 percent. In May 1986, the Senate Finance Committee unanimously approved a 27 percent rate tax bill. It would kill most tax shelters, curtail individual retirement accounts, and raise business taxes less than the House bill. The top corporate rate would be 33 percent. In June, 1986, the Senate Finance Committee's bill was passed by the Senate with only minor alterations. In August 1986, the House-Senate Conference Committee approved a compromise bill. The final tax reform bill was subsequently passed by both Houses and signed into law by President Reagan on October 22, 1986.

To facilitate this discussion of the new tax reform law and some of its likely impacts, refer to table 5–1, where many of the basic features of the tax reform law and the tax law it replaced are presented. The "old" tax law, that is, the tax law replaced by the tax reform legislation, is characterized in the third column of table 5–1; the tax reform legislation is characterized in the second column.

The old tax system (hereafter simply called *OTS*) was characterized by fourteen tax rates (fifteen for single people). As shown in table 5–1, however, the tax reform law ostensibly consists, as of 1988, of two tax rates (15 percent and 28 percent). The 15 percent tax rate would apply to all taxable income for married couples up to $29,750, whereas the 28 percent rate (which is just one percentage point above Senator Packwood's upper rate) would apply to taxable income above $29,750. For persons who are single filers, the 28 percent rate would kick in at a taxable income of $17,850. In addition to the two highly visible tax rates under the tax reform bill, there exists a *tax rate surcharge*. Under the OTS, all taxpayers—regardless of how high their income—enjoyed the benefits of lower tax rates on the "first"

Table 5–1
Tax Overhaul

Provisions	Tax Reform Law	OTS
INDIVIDUALS		
Individual tax rates	2 rates: 15% and 28%	14 rates: 11% to 50% (15 rates for single filers)
Personal exemption	$2,000 ($1,950 in 1988); phased out for taxable incomes above $149,250	$1,080
Standard Deduction	Joint filer: $5,000; head of household: $4,400; singles: $3,000	Joint filer: $3,670; head of household: $2,480; singles: $2,480
State and local taxes	Deductible except for sales taxes	Fully deductible
Charitable contributions	Deductible only for itemizers	Fully deductible for itemizers and nonitemizers

Table 5–1 continued

Provisions	Tax Reform Law	OTS
Medical deduction	Deductible in excess of 7.5% of AGI	Deductible in excess of 5% of AGI
Two-earner deduction	No	Yes
Income averaging	Not allowed	Allowed
Dividend exclusion	Repealed	$100/$200
Miscellaneous deductions	Deductible in excess of 2% of AGI	Fully deductible
Mortgage interest	Principal and second residence fully deductible; home equity loans deductible if used for home purchase, home improvement, medical or educational expenses	All mortgages, including home equity loans, fully deductible
Other interest deductions	Consumer interest not deductible; investment interest deductible up to amount equal to investment income	$10,000 plus amount equal to investment income
Individual retirement account contributions	$2,000 deductible for low- and middle-income workers; phased out for upper-middle- and high-income workers with pension plans	$2,000; $250 for nonworking spouse
401(K) Tax-deferred savings plans	Limited to $7,000 a year	Allows up to $30,000 a year
Long-term capital gains	28% top rate	20% top rate
Tax shelters	Prohibits use of losses from passive investments to offset other income	No limits on using losses from passive investment to offset other income
CORPORATIONS		
Corporate tax rate	34% top rate; 2 lower rates on income up to $75,000	46% top rate; 4 lower rates on income up to $100,000
Investment tax credit	Repealed	6% to 10%
Depreciation	Less generous than current law for equipment; much less generous for real estate	Accelerated
Manufacturing equipment	7 years, 200% front-loaded	5 years, 150% front-loaded
Commercial real estate	31.5 years, straight line	19 years, 175% front-loaded
Business meals and entertainment	80% deductible; no deduction for stadium skyboxes	Fully deductible
Oil and gas	One-year write-off for most intangible drilling costs	One-year write-off for intangible drilling costs
Bank bad debt reserves	Deductible only for banks with less than $500 million in assets	Deductible
Timber	Retains most timber write-offs	One-year write-off of most costs of growing trees

dollars of income they earned. By contrast, the tax reform law phases out the benefits of the lower (15 percent) tax rate for high-income individuals. The tax reform bill in fact places a 5 percent surcharge upon the excess of a married couple's taxable income above $71,900. For single filers, the phasing out of the 15 percent tax rate benefits begins at $43,150 worth of taxable income. Given the existence of the five percent surcharge, for 1988 and thereafter the *maximum marginal rate* of tax under the tax reform bill is then 33 percent. Furthermore, married couples face, in lieu of the 5 percent surcharge, a flat 28 percent rate on all of their taxable income if the latter exceeds $149,250.[2]

Under the tax reform bill, the personal exemption was raised from $1,080 (under the OTS) to $1,900 in 1987, to $1,950 in 1988, and to $2,000 in 1989. As of 1990, the personal exemption would be adjusted annually for inflation. However, unlike the OTS, the tax reform bill would eliminate the personal exemption for high-income taxpayers. The tax reform bill phases out the personal exemption by applying a 5 percent surcharge on joint filers with taxable incomes in excess of $149,250 up to the point where the benefits of the personal exemptions have been entirely eliminated. If the taxable income level exceeds the point where the 5 percent surcharge eliminates the benefits of the personal exemption, then the tax rate on that excess reverts back to 28 percent. Thus, as of 1988 and thereafter, the maximum marginal tax rate under any scenario is 33 percent.

Despite the phasing out of the benefits of the personal exemption for high-income family units, it is clear that the tax benefits (savings) from the personal exemption typically are greater for those in the 28 percent marginal tax bracket than for those in the 15 percent marginal tax bracket. Similarly, those whose taxable incomes places them in the first de facto 33 percent marginal bracket[3] derive relatively greater tax benefits (savings) from the personal exemption than those facing lower marginal rates. Thus, one can obviously question the personal exemption component of the tax reform bill on equity grounds. A further problem with the personal exemption aspect of the tax reform bill is that it not only is not a "simplification" for taxpayers (except those who are thereby dropped from the tax rolls) but it also will lead to a potentially significant loss of tax revenue for the Treasury. This aspect of the tax reform bill annually would cut federal tax revenues by billions of dollars. By contrast, a tax *credit* in lieu of this tax *deduction* could easily be constructed so that it still would permit dropping low income taxpayers from the tax rolls, but would sharply reduce tax revenue losses.

President Reagan had initially portrayed tax reform as being not only more equitable but also simpler than the OTS. But whether a system with two tax brackets (ostensibly) is truly a simpler system than one with fourteen (or fifteen) tax brackets is a matter of semantics. Under the OTS, when one "computed" one's taxes based upon taxable income, it was hardly necessary to peruse through a maze of fourteen (or fifteen) different tax rates. The process of determining one's taxable income was potentially arduous; after completing that task, however, computing the tax liability was very simple (albeit painful). That is, with its various tax surcharges and other provisions, one can hardly view the tax reform bill as simpler than the OTS.

As shown in Table 5–1, the tax reform bill raised (as of 1988) the standard deduction for joint filers, heads of household, and single filers. However, unlike the OTS, where the standard deduction was actually built into the tax table, the tax reform bill requires that the standard deduction be expressly subtracted from income before calculating the tax liability.

Consider next the deductibility of state and local taxes. Under the OTS, such items were fully deductible. By contrast, under Treasury II, no deduction would have been permitted for these items. For states where state plus local taxes are relatively high and where taxpayers on average also have relatively high incomes so that they are relatively likely to itemize their deductions, Treasury II's provision for total nondeductibility could present a number of problems. For example, in such high-tax states, taxpayers may suffer a disproportionately higher effective tax burden from tax reform than they would if they were to reside in relatively lower tax states. Obviously, this presents problems on equity grounds. In addition, on the basis of a number of empirical studies, including studies by Pack (1973), Cebula (1974), and Ostrosky (1978), there may be longer term implications in terms of geographic mobility: people may choose over the long run to relocate in lower tax areas. To the extent that such migration effects were manifested, there would clearly be economic ramifications in terms both of the geographic redistribution of long-term economic growth and state plus local government finance and resource problems. Moreover, cities, counties, and states may experience growing political pressure to reduce taxes (or at least to curtail the growth in taxes). This pressure is of course especially likely in those areas where the tax levels are relatively higher. This pressure may then mandate some curtailing of public services. Aside from the direct utility losses resulting from the latter curtailment, there are obvious threats to employment in the nonfederal public sector. These various political and economic considerations, combined with the aforementioned equity and migration (economic) considerations, make (in this author's view) the Treasury II proposal unpalatable in its strict form. Thus, the compromise found in the 1986 tax reform bill may be very wise. On the one hand, the nondeductibility of state and local sales taxes translates indirectly into increased (needed) revenues for the Treasury by raising taxable income. On the other hand, the continued deductibility of other state and local taxes (income taxes and property taxes) avoids the potentially very disruptive problems described earlier in this paragraph.

The tax reform bill was portrayed as eliminating or limiting many tax preferences. For example, under the OTS, charitable contributions were deductible for both itemizers and non-itemizers. Under the tax reform bill, only itemizers can deduct charitable contributions. On the one hand, this change represents, in the aggregate, only a modest dimunition in deductions. Nevertheless, it is, of and in itself, revenue-enhancing for the Treasury since it raises taxable income. Consider next the medical deduction. Under the OTS, medical expenses in excess of 5 percent of one's AGI (adjusted gross income) were deductible. Under the tax reform bill, only medical expenses in excess of 7.5 percent of one's AGI are deductible. Thus, this policy change does reduce deductions somewhat. In the aggregate, this provision will lead, of and in itself, to a modest revenue enhancement for the Treasury since it too raises taxable income. Similarly, the elimination of the two-earner deduction, of income averaging, and of the dividend exclusion, and the reduction of "miscellaneous deductions" all (1) represent a cutback in tax preferences; (2) can be viewed to some extent as tax simplifying; and (3) of and in themselves tend to be revenue-enhancing for the Treasury since they raise taxable income.

When it comes to the big items such as interest deductions, the overall reform is generally more limited. Under tax reform (as under the OTS), mortgage interest payments on first and second homes are still deductible. For most taxpayers, these interest deductions are their primary interest deductions. Thus, the "sacred cow" remains sacred. On the other hand, deductions for consumer interest payments, such as credit card interest and automobile loan interest, are to be eliminated. Interest paid on loans used to finance investments would continue to be deductible, but only as much as an amount equal to the taxpayer's investment income. The interest restrictions are being phased in over a five-year period. The tax reform bill would partially close a potential loophole that homeowners might have used to continue taking deductions for consumer interest. Interest on home loans for which the principal exceeds the amount of the purchase price of the house, plus the cost of any improvements, would not be deductible unless incurred for educational or medical expenses. To the degree that the loss of deductibility of interest payments per se stops underwriting and encouraging consumer purchases, there are two possible consequences: (1) a modest encouragement of saving and a resulting modest rise in saving, or (2) a modest decline in the incentive to spend and a resulting modest slide in consumer outlays (on new automobiles, for example). However, any projection of the net effect of these two changes on the economy or the deficit would be highly speculative, especially within the context of the dramatic and sweeping changes in the tax rate structure.

One of the more controversial aspects of the tax reform bill is its treatment of the popular IRA (individual retirement account). The tax reform bill eliminates tax deductibility for contributions to IRAs by taxpayers whose

AGI before IRA deductions exceeds $50,000 ($35,000 for single filers) and who are also covered by employers' pension plans. On the other hand, the tax reform bill retains the $2,000 deduction for all taxpayers whose income is less than $40,000 ($25,000 for individuals) and for all workers who are not covered by employer pensions. The spousal IRA deduction remains at $250. Furthermore, the tax reform bill reduces the IRA tax deduction for taxpayers who are covered by pensions and whose incomes are in the $40,000 to $50,000 range ($25,000 to $35,000 for individuals). Taxpayers precluded from making deductible IRA contributions still could make nondeductible IRA contributions of as much as $2,000 per year and could defer taxes on the interest or other earnings from the IRA.

Next, the tax reform bill sharply restricts the amount of income that can be deferred under 401(K) retirement savings plans provided by employers. The annual deferrals under 401(K) plans would be limited to $7,000, as opposed to $30,000 under the OTS. Taken together with the restrictions on IRAs, the 401(K) restrictions may to some degree discourage aggregate saving. Indeed, the IRA program was originally touted as prosaving in nature. To restrict these two programs may be to discourage saving. Given the significance of saving for financing investment in new plant and equipment, the tax reform bill provisions on IRAs and 401(K) plans may generate negative side effects for the economy over the longer run in terms of reduced capital formation and economic growth.

The tax reform bill eliminates the preferential treatment available under the OTS for long-term capital gains. Thus, income from long-term capital gains is to be taxed at the same rate as ordinary income; this provision applies to both individuals *and* corporations. Under the OTS, the maximum tax rate on long-term capital gains was 20 percent. Tax reform advocates allege that this loss of preferential treatment for long-term capital gains would simplify tax law. Taken by itself, this policy change is potentially revenue-enhancing for the Treasury since it tends to raise taxable income. On the other hand, this proposal could have a major negative impact on real estate transactions, which, in the past, could be planned to avoid any ordinary income on the sale of property.

The tax reform bill, in many respects, attempts to prevent taxpayers from using paper losses generated by tax shelters to reduce tax liability. Investments in real estate tax shelters, cattle-feeding tax shelters, and a wide array of other such arrangements have boomed in recent years. The tax reform bill makes it clear that the end of such alleged "abuses" is on its way. The tax reform bill wipes out some of the most revered tax shelters of the OTS that have enabled investors to take paper losses from real estate and other deals as tax deductions. In theory, business executives will now be forced to make investment decisions on the basis of the economic merits of a deal—not on its tax consequences per se.

Under the tax reform law, a taxpayer would not be permitted to use "passive losses" from limited partnerships or any other businesses in which the taxpayer does not materially participate to offset income from other sources, such as salary income. Such losses could be used only to offset income from other similar passive investments. Allegedly, under the provision, the tax reform bill is expected to raise Treasury tax collections by some $20 billion over the 1987 to 1991 period.

Additionally, all rental income, including but not restricted to real estate, would become subject to the loss-limitation rule, regardless of whether the taxpayer participates in managing the property. Under a special exemption, however, as much as $25,000 of losses on rental real estate could be used each year by people who actively participate in the rental activity and whose AGI is less than $100,000. If a person's AGI exceeds $100,000, then the $25,000 allowance would be reduced by 50 percent of the amount by which the AGI exceeds $100,000.

The tough rule on tax shelters would likely be a heavy blow to the real estate industry, which frequently finances development through limited-partnership arrangements that provide tax losses to investors, especially during the early years of a project. However, it would also hit many others who probably do not consider their investments to be tax shelters per se. For instance, a person who invests in a business but does not participate in its operations on a regular, continuous, and substantial basis would be unable to use losses to offset other income.

It should be noted that senators from various of the oil-producing states have carved out a special exemption for people with "working interest" investments in oil and gas drilling operations that are generally somewhat more risky than investments in real estate tax shelters. Those people still would be able to use their losses to shelter other income, even if they do not participate regularly in the drilling activity.

Finally, it should also be noted that, in order to ease its immediate effect, the tax shelter provision of the tax reform bill is phased in over a period of five years. Specifically, only 35 percent of losses would be disallowed in 1987; 60 percent would be disallowed in 1988; 80 percent would be disallowed in 1989; 90 percent would be disallowed in 1990; and 100 percent would be disallowed in 1991.

Next, consider the case of the corporate tax rates. Under the OTS, the corporate tax rate was graduated, with a 46 percent top rate. Under Treasury II, the corporate tax rate would have been graduated, with a top rate of 33 percent. As shown in table 5–1, according to the 1986 tax reform bill, the corporate tax rate is graduated, with a 34 percent top rate and two lower rates on net income up to $75,000. Thus, the top rate for business came down from 46 percent to 34 percent, marking the first time in U.S. history that the top rate for individuals is lower than the top corporate rate. Overall, although the corporate tax rate per se would be lower under the tax reform bill than under the OTS, the tax reform bill would allegedly raise aggregate corporate taxes by approximately $120 billion over five years. The latter revenue would allegedly offset presumed aggregate tax reductions of $120 billion for individuals over the same period. That is, since the tax reform bill is supposed to be revenue neutral, one of the basic alleged impacts of the bill is to shift $120 billion of tax burden from consumers to businesses over five years. This shift is supposed to raise the corporate share of total taxes from just above 8 percent to about 13 percent, and reduce the individual taxpayer's share from more than 48 percent in 1982 to about 44 percent under the tax reform bill.

Whereas the tax reform bill lowers the maximum corporate income tax rate and thereby may benefit many firms and provide them with additional funds to finance new investment, this tax rate change would of course not help the nation's most besieged industries. Moreover, by lowering the corporate tax rate, the tax reform bill would encourage firms to raise "current" income and to cut back on investment in new plant and equipment.

Various aspects of the 1986 tax reform bill and its treatment of corporations may be very disruptive to segments of the economy. One such aspect is the ITC, the "investment tax credit." Included in President Reagan's 1981 mammoth tax cut bill, the ITC allowed firms to reduce tax bills by 6 to 10 percent of the value of certain investments. Under the tax reform bill, the ITC is abandoned, as shown in table 5–1. From the perspective of heavy manufacturers, the abandonment of the ITC may be the most onerous component of the tax reform bill. Many economists argue that for such industries as the steel industry, the ITC is needed to facilitate the modernization vital to offsetting the advantages of foreign competition, such as cheap labor. The loss of the ITC could have a damaging effect on heavy industry. By contrast, high technology firms would generally not lose as much from the repeal of the ITC. Overall, however, to the extent that the ITC has resulted in an increased incentive to invest, its repeal could reduce the growth rate of capital formation. Ironically, by reducing the growth rate of capital formation, the repeal of the ITC could have an impact somewhat similar to that of crowding out (see chapter 2).

As shown in table 5–1, the tax reform bill also provides accelerated, but less generous, capital depreciation allowances for plant and equipment than existing law. This may to some degree exacerbate some of the effects of the repeal of the ITC. Depreciation allowances allow firms to recover capital costs over the so-called useful life of a factory (plant) or machinery (capital equipment). A slowdown in the depreciation schedule raises the effective tax rate on income from capital goods. The less generous depreciation schedule tends to be more burdensome to the relatively more capital intensive firms. Firms that are service-oriented, high-tech, or just generally less capital intensive also would obviously be hurt, but relatively less, since depreciation is generally less important to them. In any event, this provision of the tax reform bill would, at least to some degree, discourage capital formation, thusly adding to the potential negative effects of repealing the ITC.

Table 5–1 also shows, among other things, a very dramatic adverse change in the depreciation allowance on real estate. Surely, this will have an adverse impact on the real estate industry. Thus, there are several provisions in the tax reform bill (such as the loss of preferential capital gains treatment and the tough new treatment of tax shelters) that tend to impact adversely upon the real estate sector. The potentially stimulating impact of lower individual tax rates will offset these impacts to some degree.

Overall, to the extent that real estate becomes less attractive to investors, investment in and construction of new real estate will decline. In time, shortages of housing and other real estate forms could well develop. Rents would then skyrocket, and a comeback in the real estate industry—at a much higher average rent level—would occur.

Table 5–1 contains other items that deserve brief attention. For instance, the tax reform bill limits the deductibility of business meals and entertainment. Clearly, this provision tends to raise corporate taxable income. The limitation on the deductibility of bank bad debt reserves also tends to elevate taxable income. Note that the oil and gas and timber industries are largely protected. Nevertheless, on the whole, the lower corporate tax rates (which would otherwise *lower* tax *revenues*) are accompanied by a variety of changes, such as the repeal of the ITC, restricted depreciation allowances, restricted deductions for business meals and entertainment, and restricted deductions for bank bad debt reserves, that *increase taxable* income and hence *raise* tax *revenues* (liabilities).

A number of brief observations are now in order. To begin with, the Reagan administration has viewed the tax reform bill as a victory for conservative philosophy. The plan was based on the notion that lower tax rates for individuals will result in increased investment and increased economic growth. In many respects, the tax reform bill constitutes a retreat from the use of the federal tax code for economic and social engineering. The tax reform bill cuts back many, but certainly not all, of the tax credits and deductions now riddling the code. And it reduces the top tax rate so sharply that many of the remaining breaks lose much of their attraction. The tax reform bill also reduced the tax code's traditional tilt in favor of "smokestack" industries. In many respects, the tax reform bill also constitutes, in effect, an extremely major form of antipoverty legislation. During the last fifteen years or so, inflation and rising Social Security taxes have caused the tax burden of the poor to rise dramatically. The tax reform bill will offset much of that increase. For example, an estimated six million so-called impoverished people will be dropped from the tax rolls.

Going further, an important aspect of this allegedly revenue neutral reform bill is the shift of $120 billion in tax burden from individuals to corporations. But do corporations really pay taxes? Many analysts over the years have argued that corporations ultimately will pass on their tax burden to consumers, through reduced dividends and/or through higher retail prices in the marketplace. Next, given the myriad changes in the tax code under the tax reform bill, what happens to one's state or local income tax liabilities? The tax reform bill has cut back on a number of deductions and, although lowering federal tax rates, has also raised taxable income for most taxpayers. State and local governments using the taxable income definition in the Internal Revenue Code will thusly see a sharp rise in the tax base. Unless these state and local governments lower their tax rates, the outcome will likely be a sharp rise in state and local tax liabilities, a rise that will partially offset the alleged federal tax cut.

Next, consider the impact of the tax reform bill on investments such as municipal bonds. In this case, lower tax rates may make municipal bonds (which are exempt from federal income taxation) somewhat less attractive since they may yield a smaller tax benefit (savings). In addition, under the tax reform bill, commercial banks can no longer deduct (for purposes of computing taxable income) interest payments on deposits that are used to purchase municipal bonds. This too may dampen the demand for these bonds. On the other hand, this impact may be entirely eliminated by the fact that tax free bonds ("munis") remain one of the few largely intact tax shelters still available. In other words, given that so many other tax shelters have been wiped out, the munis begin to look better. On balance, munis may actually become more appealing than before.

Overall, the total net impact of the tax reform bill is difficult to assess. To some degree, it does appear to be a simpler system than the OTS. Depending upon one's viewpoint, it may or may not be more equitable than the OTS. In view of its repeal of the ITC and its enactment of less generous depreciation allowances, the tax reform bill may have a negative impact upon investment. On the other hand, a system of somewhat more evenhanded taxes may permit market forces to better channel investment funds in more productive directions. In addition, lower corporate tax rates should provide some firms with additional funds to finance more investment. The limitations on IRAs and 401(K) plans may have a negative impact on saving. In addition, since the biggest cut in the federal personal income tax is at the low end of the income spectrum, where the marginal propensity to consume out of current income is the highest, the tax reform bill and its alleged five-year personal income tax cut are likely to be more proconsumption that prosaving. But the sharp reduction in marginal rates overall may still lead to increased savings. Finally, it seems apparent that the tax reform bill will not—of and in itself—profoundly reduce the deficit. Of course, with the tax rates ostensibly much lower than under the OTS, it may now be easier to enact a tax increase!

Government Spending Policies

There are of course a large number of proposals for slashing the deficit through various government spending cuts.[4] Most such proposals focus upon two major areas: defense spending and domestic (nondefense) spending. Defense spending shall be briefly discussed first. Next, nondefense spending and the whole concept of congressional spending cuts will be briefly referred to.[5]

According to the Congressional Budget Office (CBO), appropriations requests by the Reagan administration for national defense programs will rise from $323 billion in budget authority in FY 1986 to $488 billion in budget authority in FY 1990, for a five-year total of about $2 trillion. Of course, these are budget requests and are thus subject to all of the impacts of the political process, including the impact (potential) of the 1985 Gramm-Rudman-Hollings Act, which shall be discussed shortly.

In certain respects, it may be helpful to view the defense budget as a large pie, a pie to be cut up into fifty slices, one for each state. To get a "feel" for the size of those slices, the reader should refer to table 5–2. Table 5–2 indicates FY 1985 defense spending in each of the states on two bases: total current dollar outlays in each state and per capita current dollar outlays in each state. As shown, California received the largest share of the total defense spending ($41.0 billion), whereas Virginia received the highest per capita level of defense spending ($2,437.00).

Among other things, table 5–2 implies that the defense budget is very unevenly distributed among the fifty states, both in terms of total dollar outlays and on a per capita basis. Thus, certain states have a far greater stake in the size and disposition of the defense budget than others. Politically, this translates into vehement opposition in Congress on the part of a number of states, many of which have large populations and a correspondingly large representation in the House, to defense cutbacks.

As for nondefense spending, emotions run high on a broad spectrum of programs. Nondefense outlays involve such diverse expenditures as those for income security; health; veterans' benefits and services; education, training and employment; social security and medicare; natural resources and the environment; energy; agriculture; community and regional development; science, space, and technology; the administration of justice; mass transit; highways; housing assistance; and international affairs. The political web in which members of Congress find themselves is indeed very tangled and complex. Resistance to change is predictable; resistance to reductions in specific programs is also predictable, perhaps more so.

Table 5–2
FY 1985 Defense Spending, by State
(in current dollars)

State	Per Capita Spending	Total Spending (billions)
Virginia	$2,437	13.9
Hawaii	2,429	2.6
Alaska	2,215	1.2
Connecticut	1,917	6.1
Missouri	1,750	8.8
Maryland	1,608	7.1
California	1,555	41.0
Massachusetts	1,471	8.6
Washington	1,351	6.0
Kansas	1,202	2.9
Maine	1,138	1.3
New Hampshire	1,083	1.1
Georgia	1,061	6.3
Texas	1,006	16.5
Utah	986	1.6
Arizona	983	3.1
Colorado	945	3.1
New Mexico	874	1.3
Florida	856	9.7
Mississippi	851	2.2
Alabama	794	3.2
Rhode Island	793	0.8
South Carolina	789	2.6
Delaware	729	0.5
Indiana	719	4.0
Louisiana	707	3.2
New Jersey	706	5.3
North Dakota	705	0.5
Oklahoma	651	2.1
New York	638	11.3
Minnesota	614	2.6
North Carolina	613	3.8
Ohio	589	6.3
Arkansas	582	1.4
Nevada	554	0.5
Pennsylvania	536	6.4
Wyoming	507	0.3
Kentucky	465	1.7
Nebraska	438	0.7
Vermont	414	0.2
Michigan	396	3.6
South Dakota	359	0.3
Tennessee	329	1.6
Montana	323	0.3
Illinois	295	3.4
Wisconsin	293	1.4
Idaho	273	0.3
Iowa	260	0.7
Oregon	220	0.6
West Virginia	126	0.2

Source: Economic Report of the President, 1986, Table B–76.

In the face of various forms of powerful resistance to reductions in both defense and nondefense outlays, can the Gramm-Rudman-Hollings Act, with its various provisions for reducing the federal deficit, really work to restore what some refer to as fiscal responsibility? It is possible, but it seems most unlikely, especially in view of the July 1986 Supreme Court ruling that the provision in this legislation for automatic spending cuts is unconstitutional.

Members of Congress and the president are well aware that numerous programs have outlived their basic function and that they should consequently be terminated. Nevertheless, the political process has resulted in few terminations. Indeed, the *President's Private Sector Survey on Cost Control* (Grace Commission, 1984, p. 5) "found congressional interference to be a problem. For example, because Congress obstructs the closing of bases that (even) the military wants to close, the three-year waste is $367 million." President Reagan, for all of his rhetoric in favor of spending cuts, has provided only a modicum of actual cuts. Indeed, it has been during his terms in office that aggregate federal spending and deficits (in nominal and real terms) have risen so rapidly. Although the president attempts to place the blame on Congress, the actual facts do not entirely support his allegations. In point of fact, Congress has allocated more for social programs than the president wanted; however, Congress has simultaneously allocated less for defense spending. The result is that, for example, for the period FY 1982 through FY 1984, Congress spent about $60 billion above the aggregate budget requested by the president. And that $60 billion represents only 11.5 percent of the aggregate budget deficits accumulated for those same three fiscal years.

In 1981, President Reagan successfully obtained congressional approval of over $35 billion in spending cuts. Subsequent efforts at such deep cuts have failed. It may be that, when Congress is voting on individual programs, all it directly feels is the pressure from special interest groups; perhaps Congress feels no simultaneous and consistent offsetting pressure from taxpayers.

Moreover, Congress and the president have always liked to play "number games." These number games take a number of forms. One form involves announcing that one has achieved a "savings" of X billions of dollars on a program, when in reality if an investigation of the facts is undertaken, it can be shown that spending within the program in question has actually risen by Y billions of dollars over the previous year's level. Why can politicians get away with such misleading rhetoric? The reason is that the approved program *is* actually X billions of dollars less than the initial budget request!

But there are more misleading (if not more dangerous) forms of number games that members of Congress, presidents, and others play. One of the most abused is that of inflating estimates of "needed" spending and/or of expected revenues. Committee chairpersons commonly submit inflated estimates of spending needs to the budget committee since each of these committee chairpersons generally wants to maximize his or her committee's allocation. Moreover, the budget committee itself is capable of intentionally inflating or deflating: they frequently underestimate certain categories of outlays and overestimate expected revenue receipts. The outcome can be approval of a relatively meaningless budget resolution.

Theoretically, the Gramm-Rudman-Hollings Act is meant to deal directly and strongly with the so-called deficit problem. This legislation provides a blueprint for cutting the deficit, over a five-year period, down to zero by 1991. According to the Gramm-Rudman-Hollings Act, if the deficit is not cut or cut sufficiently by the Congress (and the president), then automatic budget reductions will occur in an across-the-board fashion.

At first blush, this legislation appeared to have generated an extraordinarily powerful pressure to cut outlays and, possibly, to even elevate taxes. Unfortunately, in July 1986, the Supreme Court ruled a provision of the Gramm-Rudman-Hollings Act to be unconstitutional. This legislation had established machinery to trigger automatic spending cuts should the Congress and president fail to cut deficits to the target levels prescribed in the legislation. The Supreme Court found the automaticity of the spending cuts to be unconstitutional; otherwise, the legislation is intact and binding. Clearly, the Supreme Court has removed some of the "teeth" from this legislation. Nevertheless, at least in theory, Congress and the president must abide by the act and allegedly now bear the burden of voting for specific spending cuts rather than merely hiding behind the automatic trigger mechanism. In any event, even if the Supreme Court has merely weakened and not killed the initiative, we should not be altogether shocked if Congress amends the act—which Congress can, by a simple majority vote.

As a possible index of things to come, consider the fact that a mere one- or two-year freeze on cost-of-living adjustments (COLAs) to Social Security could easily trim tens upon tens of billions from the federal budget over the next five years. Yet, at the behest of President Reagan, Social Security was exempted from the Gramm-Rudman-Hollings Act.

It would appear that Congress's (and the president's) capacity for self-control is extremely limited. Although the Gramm-Rudman-Hollings Act may bring a temporary slowdown to the growth of federal spending and deficits, there appears to be little reason to believe that, one way or another, the impact of this legislation on the federal budget will not be very short-lived.

But what if sizable spending cuts are in fact involved? There is a potential danger, just as there was a potential danger with tax increases. Namely, depending upon the magnitude, nature, and timing of such spending cuts, either an economic slowdown or a recession could result. Ironically, the theoretical gains towards deficit reduction could then be partially or even totally offset by reduced tax collections and expanded government transfers. If a policy of spending cuts, or perhaps more accurately, reduced spending growth, is undertaken, our decision makers need to be cautious as to the form, size, and timing of those cuts if they are to effectively pursue deficit reduction. Recession and/or a larger deficit problem could arise.

Monetary Policy

Just a brief mention of the potential role of monetary policy may be in order. If a coordinated effort between monetary policy decision makers and fiscal decision makers occurs, it would seem at least plausible for progress towards deficit reduction to be made with a relative minimum of adverse effects to the economy as a whole.

Potentially, an effectively executed, expansionary monetary policy could be combined with a very cautious, moderate policy of deficit reduction by the Congress and the president. If monetary expansion were sufficiently strong, interest rates could be pushed downwards. In turn, consumer spending and investment spending would presumably rise, pushing upwards upon the GNP level. The latter impact would in turn act to elevate tax collections (and perhaps to reduce government transfers). With downward pressure on interest rates, government debt service requirements for new and refinanced debt would also decline. Moreover, with a lower interest rate structure, the value of the dollar might be depressed enough to somewhat elevate exports and reduce imports. This improvement in the balance of trade might in turn push upwards on GNP and hence tax collections. Of course, these are only possible, and indeed optimistic, forecasts. Nevertheless, it is entirely conceivable that the above sequence of events, or some reasonable facsimile thereof, would not only directly act to reduce the deficit per se, but might also permit sufficient growth in the economy to offset the potentially depressing effects on the economy as a whole of genuine deficit reduction policies by the Congress and the president.

Of course, such a scenario is possible, but not necessarily very probable. For instance, how expansionary should the monetary policy be? If excessively expansionary, inflation problems and inflationary expectations could severely or totally undermine policy effectiveness. Moreover, if an expansionary monetary policy acts to reduce interest rates, just how low and how rapidly can they fall? There are limits! And, if would-be borrowers come to perceive a policy of more or less continuous interest rate drops, they may come to expect future interest rate drops and thus may postpone borrowing and the spending it might finance. Similar expectations on the part of lenders may further complicate the picture. Recessionary potential, with all that it entails, might ensue. Or, at the least, a slowdown might occur.

Overview

Chapter 2 described, in theoretical terms, the concept of crowding out, which—depending upon the theory under consideration—could be characterized as either complete, partial, or zero. Chapter 3 empirically examined whether there was evidence to substantiate the existence of a crowding out effect from deficits. In Chapter 3, it was clearly established (in this author's view) that crowding out does occur. Indeed, although the techniques adopted are entirely different, chapter 3 of this book generated conclusions that are entirely consistent with those in Cagan (1985) and Barth, Iden, and Russek (1984 and 1985), as well as an earlier study by Feldstein and Eckstein (1970). It has also been argued here that, as Cagan (1985) argues as well, although crowding out does apparently occur, it is only partial (see also Abrams and Schmitz [1978], Arestis [1979], Cebula [1985], and Zahn [1978]). That is, although it appears that deficits may carry with them some adverse side effects, there nonetheless typically may be some positive net benefits to the economy as a whole in terms of economic growth and expansion. Put differently, were the increases in public spending and private spending associated with the enormous deficits of calendar year 1982, on balance, bad? Hardly. The deficit of 1982 must in any reasonable evaluation be given at least some of the credit for pulling our economy out of the 1981–82 recession.[6] It is this author's view, then, that crowding out does occur; that it must logically only be partial; and that, on balance most deficits tend to— whether directly or indirectly—stimulate the economy to at least some degree.

The present chapter has warned of the potential dangers of combatting the deficit through tax increases or diminished government spending. In terms of the 1981–82 recession, for example, efforts to balance the federal budget in 1982 would have had very destructive consequences. Had the deficit been eradicated by either higher taxes or diminished government outlays, the outcome would have been reduced private and/or public spending, with no exodus from the recession, and quite likely a deepened (as well as prolonged) recession.

A few additional comments about the deficit and the national debt might now be in order. The current national debt is in the range of $2 trillion. Most of this debt is owned by U.S. businesses and citizens, either directly or through their financial institutions. If the federal government is in some sense poorer because it owes more, then the private sector of the economy may also be better off (richer) in terms of its holdings of Treasury debt.[7] Presumably, people who view themselves as richer have a greater propensity to spend. If this line of reasoning is valid, then a huge national debt can, through a "wealth effect," stimulate the economy. This in turn implies, once again, that although crowding out may occur (see chapter 3), there presumably are net positive benefits from federal debt and deficits.

Next, consider the role of inflation when evaluating the national debt and changes therein (deficits). Inflation alters the value of the national debt so that the size of the deficit per se exaggerates the growth of the real national debt. If the inflation occurs at a 5 percent annual rate, the real value of an existing $2 trillion debt is reduced by 5 percent, or $100 billion. With a deficit of, say, 180 billion current dollars, the total real debt rises by $180 billion less $100 billion, or "only" $80 billion (technically even less, since the deficit per se should also be deflated). A problem with deficits and the national debt may well exist, but really how big is it?

Next, consider the aforementioned wealth effect together with the effects of inflation within the context of the Gramm-Rudman-Hollings Act. In accord with this legislation, assume that the deficit is eliminated as of 1991. With zero inflation, the real value of the national debt would be unchanged in 1991. However, if there is any inflation whatsoever during 1991, the real value of the national debt will decline. This reduction in real wealth could theoretically reduce private sector purchasing power and thus private sector expenditures, and, as a result, contribute further to the adverse impacts that higher taxes or slowed federal government spending might have generated. Indeed, even if the deficit is not eliminated but is merely drastically reduced, only a modicum of inflation could theoretically yield these kinds of adverse wealth effects.

On the other hand, consider the so-called Ricardian Equivalence Theorem, as developed by Barro (1974). Stated simply this theorem argues that an increase in government debt is effectively equivalent to a future increase in tax liabilities. Accordingly, the increase in federal debt is not judged to be an addition to the stock of private wealth.

In order to gain a fundamental grasp of this view, it is technically necessary to alter the basic assumptions of the conventional life-cycle model in two ways. To begin with, one must assume that each generation receives utility not only from its own lifetime consumption per se, but from that of its offspring as well. A given generation need not take into account the utility levels of all future generations. By being concerned merely about the next generation, it is tied to all ensuing generations through a chain of interdependent utility functions. This assumption implies that the current generation will adjust its saving so as to offset fiscal actions that have impacts beyond its own lifetime. Next, also assume that the present value of government outlays must equal the present value of tax liabilities. This de facto "intertemporal budget constraint" for the government sector imposes a limitation (theoretically) on the growth of the government's debt. Government bonds issued in the current time period in order to finance a current deficit must be matched by future taxes to service and discharge the debt being accumulated.[8]

In any event, a number of empirical studies, including studies by Kormendi (1983), Seater (1982), and Tanner (1979), have found a relatively high degree of future tax liability discounting so that current federal deficits appear to have no real influence over current consumer outlays. However, these findings have been rather convincingly attacked by Reid (1985, p. 486), who finds that "permanent deficit flows exert considerable influence upon private consumption decisions."

Earlier in this book it was argued that deficits are not all good—there are adverse side effects associated with a deficit. However, it should also be clear that we must reject the mythical notion that all deficits are necessarily bad. We need not be preoccupied with deficits and the national debt. Nor, of course, should we be entirely complacent, for as Cagan (1985, p. 218) warns, the financing and economic impacts of deficits appear to be somewhat unstable, and it is unclear as to how long credit markets will be able to continue absorbing large volumes of Treasury borrowings in the future without greater adverse side effects. And, Cagan (1985, p. 218) further warns, while crowding out has to date been only moderate, "this could change."

Notes

1. See Waud (1985) regarding the self-defeating aspect of policies aimed at deficit reduction.

2. The tax reform bill provides for a "blending" of the new rates with those of the OTS for 1987.

3. This 33 percent rate consists simply of the 28 percent rate plus the 5 percent surcharge to offset 15 percent tax rate benefits for higher income people.

4. The list is altogether too lengthy to provide here. Nevertheless, the reader may find the budgetary proposals by the Heritage Foundation, edited by John Palffy (1985), of interest. Similarly, the Congressional Budget Office study (1985) is enlightening, as is the study by the Grace Commission, *The President's Private Sector Survey on Cost Control* (1984).

5. The interested reader may wish to read the paper by Laband (1983).

6. However, as evidenced by the recent paper by Liebling (1985), not all economists agree with this appraisal.

7. Holding the stock of federal government assets fixed, an increase in the debt/asset ratio will raise the value of the claims of bond holders, ceteris paribus. Impounded in ceteris paribus, of course, is the aggregate price level.

8. As Barth, Iden, and Russek (1984, p. 81) observe, in the absence of the first assumption, a tax cut would cause the current generation to raise its consumption level, thusly transferring the burden of the government debt completely onto future generations. Furthermore, in the absence of the second assumption, no one would have cause to believe that deficits are in some sense a temporary phenomenon or, moreover, that government debt would not expand indefinitely.

References

Abrams, B.A. and Schmitz, M.D. 1978. "The 'Crowding Out' Effect of Government Transfers on Private Charitable Contributions." *Public Choice* 33:29–39.

Arestis, P. 1979. " 'The Crowding Out' of Private Expenditure by Fiscal Actions: An Empirical Investigation." *Public Finance/Finances Publiques* 34:19–41.

Barro, R.J. 1974. "Are Government Bonds Net Wealth?" *Journal of Political Economy* 82:1095–1117.

Barth, J.R., Iden, G., and Russek, F.S. 1984. "Do Federal Deficits Really Matter?" *Contemporary Policy Issues* 3:79–95.

—— 1985. "Federal Borrowing and Short-Term Interest Rates: Comment." *Southern Economic Journal* 50:554–59.

Cagan, P. 1985. *The Economy in Deficit*. Washington, D.C.: American Enterprise Institute.

Cebula, R.J. 1974. "Local Government Policies and Migration: An Analysis for SMSAs in the United States." *Public Choice* 19:86–93.

—— 1985. "Crowding Out and Fiscal Policy in the United States: A Note on the Recent Experience." *Public Finance/Finances Publiques* 40:133–36.

Evans, P. 1985. "Do Large Deficits Produce High Interest Rates?" *American Economic Review* 75:68–87.

Feldstein, M. and Eckstein, O. 1970. "The Fundamental Determinants of the Interest Rate." *Review of Economics and Statistics* 52:363–75.

Grace Commission. 1984. *President's Private Sector Survey on Cost Control*. Washington, D.C.: U.S. Government Printing Office.

Hoelscher, G. 1983. "Federal Borrowing and Short Term Interest Rates." *Southern Economic Journal* 50:319–33.

King, A. 1978. "The American Polity in the Late 1970s: Building Coalitions in the Sand." In *The New American Political System*, ed. by Anthony King, 371–96. Washington, D.C. American Enterprise Institute.

Kormendi, R.C. 1983. "Government Debt, Government Spending, and Private Sector Behavior." *American Economic Review* 73:994–1010.

Laband, D.N. 1983. "Federal Budget Cuts: Bureaucrats Trim the Meat, Not the Fat." *Public Choice* 41:311–14.

Liebling, H.I. 1985. "The Myth of the Keynesian Recovery." *Journal of Macroeconomics* 7:257–60.

Makin, J.H. 1983. "Real Interest, Money Surprises, Anticipated Inflation and Fiscal Deficits." *Review of Economics and Statistics* 65:374–84.

Mascaro, A. and Meltzer, A.H. 1983. "Long- and Short-Term Interest Rates in a Risky World." *Journal of Monetary Economics* 10:485–518.

Motley, B. 1983. "Real Interest Rates, Money, and Government Deficits." *Federal Reserve Bank of San Francisco Economic Review* Summer: 31–45.

Ostrosky, A. 1978. "Some Economic Effects and Causes of State and Local Government Commitment to Public Education." *Review of Business and Economic Research* 14:68–72.

Pack, J.R. 1973. "Determinants of Migration to Central Cities." *Journal of Regional Science* 13:249–60.

Palffy, J., ed. 1985. *How to Slash $119 Billion from the Deficit*. Washington, D.C.: The Heritage Foundation.

Reese, T.J. 1980. *The Politics of Taxation*. Westport, Conn.: Quorum Books.

Reid, B. 1985. "Aggregate Consumption and Deficit Financing: An Attempt to Separate Permanent from Transitory Effects." *Economic Inquiry* 23:475–86.

Seater, J. 1982. "Are Future Taxes Discounted?" *Journal of Money, Credit, and Banking* 14:376–89.

Stockman, D. 1986. *The Triumph of Politics*. New York: Harper and Row.

Surrey, S. 1957. "The Congress and the Tax Lobbyist—How Special Tax Provisions Get Enacted." *Harvard Law Review* 70:1145–82.

Tanner, J.E. 1979. "Fiscal Policy and Consumer Behavior." *Review of Economics and Statistics* 61:317–21.

U.S. Congress. Congressional Budget Office. 1985. *Reducing the Deficit: Spending and Revenue Options*. Washington, D.C.: U.S. Government Printing Office.

Waud, R.N. 1985. "Politics, Deficits, and the Laffer Curve." *Public Choice* 47:509–17.

Zahn, F. 1978. "A Flow of Funds Analysis of Crowding Out." *Southern Economic Journal* 45:195–206.

Index

About the Author

Richard J. Cebula is professor of economics at Emory University. He received his A.B. degree from Fordham College and his Ph.D. degree from Georgia State University. Dr. Cebula has published numerous articles in major scholarly journals in the fields of migration, regional economics, and macroeconomics. He also is the author of *The Determinants of Human Migration* (1979), *Geographic Living-Cost Differentials* (1983), and *The Federal Budget Deficit: An Economic Analysis* (1986), all published by Lexington Books.

HJ 2052 .C42 1987

Cebula, Richard J.

The deficit problem in
  perspective

A113 0897642 9